Richar

T0044961

The Case for a
Debt Jubilee

polity

The right of Richard Vague to be identified as Author of this Work has been asserted in accordance with the UK Copyright, Designs and Patents Act 1988.

First published in 2022 by Polity Press

Polity Press
65 Bridge Street
Cambridge CB2 1UR, UK

Polity Press
101 Station Landing
Suite 300
Medford, MA 02155, USA

ISBN-13: 978-1-5095-4872-9
ISBN-13: 978-1-5095-4873-6 (pb)

A catalogue record for this book is available from the British Library.

Library of Congress Cataloging-in-Publication Data

Names: Vague, Richard, author.
Title: The case for a debt jubilee / Richard Vague.
Description: Cambridge, UK ; Medford, MA : Polity Press, 2022. | Includes bibliographical references. | Summary: "How we can stave off economic disaster by freeing millions from debt bondage"-- Provided by publisher.
Identifiers: LCCN 2021017322 (print) | LCCN 2021017323 (ebook) | ISBN 9781509548729 (hardback) | ISBN 9781509548736 (paperback) | ISBN 9781509548743 (epub)
Subjects: LCSH: Debt relief. | Loans, Personal. | Debts, Public. | Financial crises.
Classification: LCC HG3755.3 .V34 2022 (print) | LCC HG3755.3 (ebook) | DDC 332.024/02--dc23
LC record available at https://lccn.loc.gov/2021017322
LC ebook record available at https://lccn.loc.gov/2021017323

Typeset in 11 on 15pt Sabon by
Cheshire Typesetting Ltd, Cuddington, Cheshire
Printed and bound in Great Britain by CPI Group (UK) Ltd, Croydon

For further information on Polity, visit our website:
politybooks.com

Contents

1

High Levels of Private Debt Stifle the Economy

In many of the most prominent ancient civilizations, including ancient Sumer, Babylon, Assyria, Akkadia, Egypt, Sparta, Corinth, and China, excessive household debt was a huge and recurring problem. This may come as a surprise to a reader today, because ancient societies are often misleadingly described as barter-based. In fact, debt was a necessary and pervasive part of these earliest economies, and our ancient ancestors quickly developed a sophisticated understanding of debt and lending, with laws and institutions to govern that lending. Debt did then many of the same things that it does now: it facilitated payment for labor, allowed for the acquisition of supplies, and bridged the time between planting and harvest – the reaping and then the sowing of profit.

Some families in these agricultural societies would

find themselves with little option but to amass debts in order to live, but in time the burden of this debt could cause them to lose their land, their means of sustenance, and even their liberty, in the tragic form of debt bond servitude. This debt accumulated as unpaid bills, starting with fees and taxes owed to the king; debts to ale houses; and debts to the government for farming supplies. Interest rates were high and lenders quickly learned the power of compounding. Bouts of disease, drought, war, or other disasters often exacerbated citizens' debt burdens. These ancient economies would sometimes reach the brink of collapse under the staggering weight of private indebtedness.

For this reason among others, kings devised the practice of debt forgiveness or amnesty as a solution. A king might proclaim a debt amnesty for a number of reasons, as we will see, including to ensure that citizens were available to serve in his army and help build the great public works of that society. At first, historians were surprised to learn of this phenomenon, but archeologically documented instances of debt amnesty are numerous and growing, and refer to actual, and fundamental, debt practices in these cultures. In fact, some historians view this practice as conservative, counterintuitive as that may sound, since it was a mechanism that both preserved the practice of lending and kept those loans from over-whelming these economies.

A key Old Testament passage, Deuteronomy 15:2–3, describes clearly the time when these debt amnesties were proclaimed: "Every creditor shall cancel any loan they have made to a fellow Israelite. They shall not require payment from anyone among their own people, because the LORD's time for can-celling debts has been proclaimed. You may require payment from a foreigner, but you must cancel any debt your fellow Israelite owes you."

Just as lending is almost as old as civilization, so, too, is predatory lending. The modern Rabbinical scholar Jacob Milgrom writes in *Leviticus 17–22* that King Urukagina of Lagash (c. 2400 BCE), one of the first enactors of debt amnesty, saw that "offi-cials stole property and land from citizens, forced them to sell their houses, demanded exorbitant rates for essential services, [and] imposed unjust taxes. Impoverished farmers and artisans became indentured servants."

Debt amnesty was easiest in the earliest civiliza-tions, when lenders were primarily the palace and the temple, since the government was simply for-giving debt it had extended to its citizens. Many of these ancient debts were not loans so much as arrears: an accrual of tax or other obligations that citizens could not pay. But over time, large merchants and landowners became significant lenders, too, and acts of debt amnesty also required that these lenders forgive debts. If by his own debt amnesty proclamation the king forgave a loan his office had extended, it was a loss borne by that king. If by proclamation the king forced other lenders to forgive debts, it was a loss borne by those lenders.

Debt amnesty typically would cancel agrarian debts owed by the citizenry at large, return land that had been lost due to unpaid debt, and liberate bondservants, who were often family members pledged as collateral for loans. Amnesty was limited and enacted only occasionally. It applied to the debt of owner-occupants alone and wasn't for the rich or for businessmen's mercantile debts, so in a sense ancient debt amnesties were "means tested." Economist and historian Michael Hudson, one of the very few to predict the 2008 financial crisis, has studied ancient debt extensively, and I draw on his work here. He explains, "Only subsistence landholdings were returned to the customary holders, not townhouses and other wealth over and above the basic subsistence needs of citizens. So the aim was not equality as such, but the assurance of self-support land and production for the citizenry."

High Levels of Private Debt Stifle the Economy

These civilizations used terms such as "return" and "straightening out" to describe debt amnesty, and the objective, as Hudson writes, was to ensure that each family had the land and resources they needed for sustenance, unburdened by debt. The act meshed with these societies' prevailing idea of cyclical time rather than linear time. With debt amnesty, everyone could return to land that their family had once owned but lost to a lender. Family members lost to debt bondage returned home, and the family was given a new, debt-free beginning. This cyclical paradigm, of course, mirrored the cycles of planting and harvest that formed the sole context of their lives. *Things always ended. Things always had to begin again.* (Superficially, the idea of time and debt as cyclical and renewing instead of linear lingers today with modern sports teams, which start each season with a clean slate of no wins or losses.)

Proclamations of debt amnesty were ad hoc, but often announced at the beginning of a king's reign. Most members of Hammurabi's Babylonian dynasty, for example, inaugurated their rule with a new proclamation of debt amnesty. One Babylonian king issued four acts of debt amnesty during his forty-year reign. An invading king could promise debt amnesty to a city's inhabitants to entice them to side with him and turn on their ruler. By the same token, an incumbent king could use debt amnesty to keep a population from siding with an invader.

The ancient Israelites took debt relief an important step further: they removed it from the realm of a king's whims and encoded it into their laws, making it recur the year after every seven cycles of seven years. Debt relief changed from an ad hoc to a structural aspect of the economy. The Israelites called it Jubilee, after the ram's horn, or *yobel* (featured on the cover of this book), that was sounded for the joyous proclamation of this freedom from the burden of debt.

Jubilee brought liberation from debt and a restoration and renewal of these societies and economies.

The Private Debt Problem in the Twenty-First Century

Today, we find ourselves with a similar private sector debt accumulation problem, and the idea of strategic debt amnesty or jubilee is arguably more urgent than ever. We were drowning in debt before the Covid-19 crisis, and now we are deluged by it.

"Total debt," as it will be used in this book, means the sum of public and private sector debt, and private sector debt is comprised of business and household debt, including student loans, mortgages, auto loans, small business loans, credit card debt, and more. In 1951, total debt stood at 128 percent of US national GDP. By the end of 2019, this figure had doubled to 258 percent (see Chart 1). Government debt has also increased markedly and gets the most attention, but we should be more concerned about the rapid growth in private sector debt. From 1951 to 2019, US government debt grew from 74 percent to 108 percent of GDP, but US private sector debt grew even faster, almost tripling from 54 percent to 150 percent. Private debt is necessary and can boost economic growth, but high debt levels, whether for individuals or businesses or both, burden and stunt this growth.

As both the government and American households and businesses used debt to fight the economic collapse caused by the Covid-19 pandemic, these debt ratios continued to spike. From December 2019 to December 2020, total private debt surged by $2.1 trillion, from 150 to 164 percent of annual GDP, making the climb back from the damage all the more arduous, while government debt grew from 108 to 133 percent.

Private debt has almost always been a larger and more consequential factor than government debt in economic outcomes, if for no other reason than

Chart 1

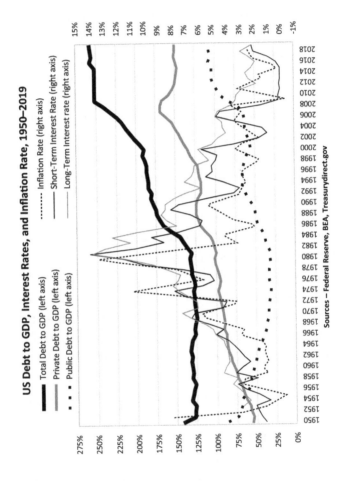

US Debt to GDP, Interest Rates, and Inflation Rate, 1950–2019

— Total Debt to GDP (left axis)
— Private Debt to GDP (left axis)
...... Public Debt to GDP (right axis)

...... Inflation Rate (right axis)
— Short-Term Interest Rate (right axis)
— Long-Term Interest rate (right axis)

Sources – Federal Reserve, BEA, Treasurydirect.gov

its sheer magnitude. Globally, in countries that together total 90 percent of all GDP, public debt totals roughly $70 trillion, while private sector debt totals $123 trillion. GDP growth in developed countries is also more closely correlated to private sector than public sector debt growth.

Since GDP is essentially a measurement of our national income, the ratio of private debt to GDP is the national equivalent of the "debt-to-income" ratio a lender uses when they evaluate your application for a car loan or a mortgage. The higher the ratio, the heavier your debt burden. Debt growth is generally faster than GDP growth in developed economies, and this state of affairs is referred to as "financialization" or "financial deepening."

Financialization has been lauded by some economists as the hallmark of a mature economy, but it is, to the contrary, the very thing that eventually overburdens households and businesses with debt and slows an economy. For major countries whose governments have "monetary sovereignty" – that is, countries that control their own monetary system, create their own money, and borrow in their own currency – government debt is far less likely to end with default. That's because those governments can create money to pay back public debts. But households and businesses have no such luxury, and thus private debt is much more likely to default.

It's not just a problem in the United States (see Charts 2 through 5). From 1990 to 2019 in China, the private (non-central government) sector debt-to-GDP ratio rocketed from 87 percent to 204 percent of GDP and total debt from 94 percent to 260 percent of GDP. Taking the five largest European countries together – Germany, France, the United Kingdom, Spain, and Italy – private sector debt increased from 80 percent of GDP in 1970 to 149 percent in 2019, while in that same period total debt grew from 108 to 238 percent (though within this, the distribution is tilted to the benefit of Germany because of its huge net export advantage). In Japan, from 1964 to 2019, the total private debt-to-GDP ratio grew from 118 to 163 percent, including a huge private debt growth spike that brought the banking crisis of the 1990s. The country's total debt in this period grew from 123 to 402 percent of GDP.

Collectively, these countries tell the overall global story, since they constitute 60 percent of world GDP and 75 percent of the world's debt. The debt problem, especially the private debt subset of that problem, is global but concentrated in the larger, developed countries. Developing countries tend to have lower total debt-to-GDP ratios, but even in

Chart 2

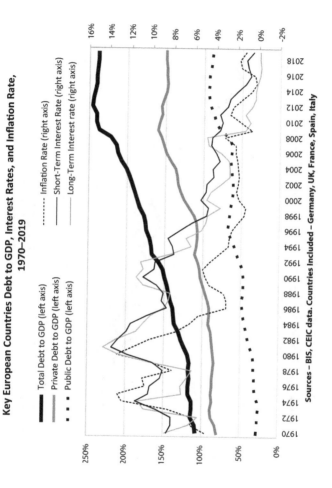

Key European Countries Debt to GDP, Interest Rates, and Inflation Rate, 1970–2019

Total Debt to GDP (left axis)
Private Debt to GDP (left axis)
Public Debt to GDP (left axis)
Inflation Rate (right axis)
Short-Term Interest Rate (right axis)
Long-Term Interest rate (right axis)

Sources – BIS, CEIC data. Countries Included – Germany, UK, France, Spain, Italy

Chart 3

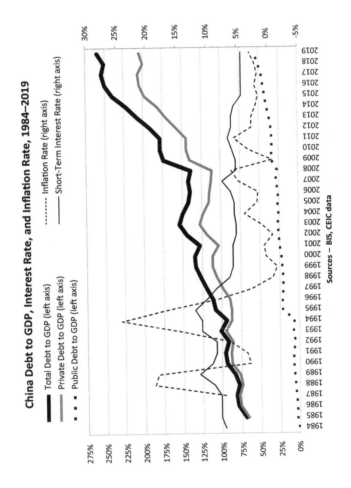

China Debt to GDP, Interest Rate, and Inflation Rate, 1984–2019

Total Debt to GDP (left axis)
Private Debt to GDP (left axis)
Public Debt to GDP (left axis)
Inflation Rate (right axis)
Short-Term Interest Rate (right axis)

Sources – BIS, CEIC data

Chart 4

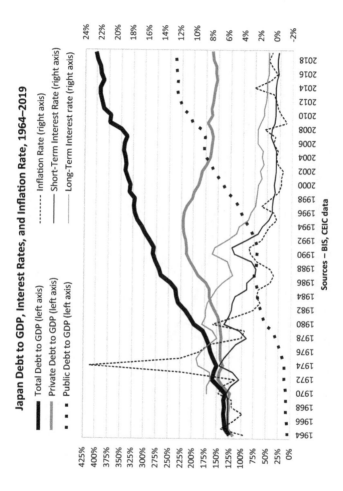

Japan Debt to GDP, Interest Rates, and Inflation Rate, 1964–2019

— Total Debt to GDP (left axis)
······· Inflation Rate (right axis)
— Private Debt to GDP (left axis)
— Short-Term Interest Rate (right axis)
■ ■ Public Debt to GDP (left axis)
— Long-Term Interest rate (right axis)

Sources – BIS, CEIC data

Chart 5

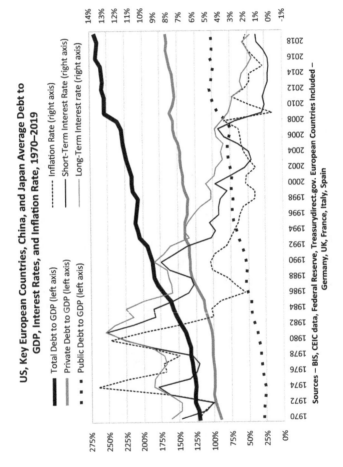

US, Key European Countries, China, and Japan Average Debt to GDP, Interest Rates, and Inflation Rate, 1970–2019

- Total Debt to GDP (left axis)
- Private Debt to GDP (left axis)
- Public Debt to GDP (left axis)
- Inflation Rate (right axis)
- Short-Term Interest Rate (right axis)
- Long-Term Interest rate (right axis)

Sources – BIS data, CEIC data, Federal Reserve, Treasurydirect.gov. European Countries Included – Germany, UK, France, Italy, Spain a developing country such as India, the trend is clear. From 1951 to 2019, India's private sector debt grew from 22 to 87 percent of GDP, and total debt from 47 to 159 percent. (A detailed analysis of these other countries is beyond the scope of this book, which is focused on the United States.)

In the United States today, private sector loans are asphyxiating many households and businesses. The debt burden for individuals in almost every age group and for businesses of every size is increasing. In my investigations of household debt, it has not been uncommon to find families with all of the following: mortgage debt as great as or greater than the value of their home; student loans still outstanding for the parents; and large debts tied to some unexpected healthcare expense. A growing number of economists decry our slowing long-term growth rate as "secular stagnation." They explain it as a structural slowdown from such factors as a chronic lack of demand, without recognizing the rising burden of private sector debt as a basic culprit in that stagnation. Families with high debt are far less able to pay for their own children's college, build additions to their homes, buy appliances, or start new businesses – the very types of things that power an economy forward. Likewise, small businesses that carry too much debt are far less likely to expand, add product lines, or invest in research and development. This huge debt overhang portends an extended period of stagnant and ever-slower economic growth with falling living standards for millions of debt-burdened households.

Not only is the high burden of private debt a deeply consequential problem in its own right, it has also been an underlying issue in several of our recent, and worst, social and economic problems. Runaway household mortgage debt growth brought the 2008 global crisis. The ensuing slow GDP growth largely resulted from the residual burden of this crisis debt, and some commentators believe it helped kindle the discontent that led to Donald Trump's election in 2016. Since minority communities have disproportionately felt the private debt burden, it has also exacerbated the racial injustice that has only become more urgent and visible in the 2020s. High debt, along with unemployment and underemployment, has contributed to our opioid crisis. As we will see, it deepens inequality. And this debt will hobble our efforts to move the economy forward from the pandemic.

High Levels of Private Debt Stifle the Economy

High Private Debt Is a Harmfully Consequential and Yet Largely Ignored Problem

Private debt has enormous effects on American economic and societal trends – and yet it is not central to the most widely used economic forecasting models. Some economists have downplayed the adverse effect of this dramatic increase in household debt in part because they maintain that the decline in overall interest rates has offset it. To be sure, lower interest rates have helped many debtors immensely, especially mortgage holders, who have repeatedly refinanced to lower rates. But the debt service burden on households is still alarming, even accounting for lower rates. Though it has come down to some extent very recently, the "debt service ratio," which estimates the payments consumers make on their debt in relation to their income, is still roughly 30 percent higher now than it was in the 1950s and 1960s, the two most vibrant growth decades in the post-World War II era (see Chart 6). It's no coincidence that our highest-growth decades since World War II came when households had their lowest debt service burden. The debt payment ratio story is similar for business.

This is the vicious dynamic at the heart of working Americans' financial distress. Higher debt curbs

	1950s	1960s	1970s	1980s	1990s	2000s	2050s
Private Debt to GDP (average)	64%	85%	95%	111%	122%	153%	151%
Real GDP Growth (average)	4.3%	4.5%	3.2%	3.1%	3.2%	1.9%	2.3%
Real GDP Per capita Growth (average)	2.4%	3.2%	2.2%	2.2%	2.0%	0.9%	1.6%

Sources – BEA, Federal Reserve, Census

Chart 6

spending, which constrains growth. Constrained growth suppresses wages. Lower wages further constrain spending and growth. And lower wages contribute to one of the most problematic and most dire examples of private debt today as a symptom of economic dysfunction: the extent to which Americans who have seen their wages stagnate over recent decades rely on debt to meet their basic needs.

Some mainstream economists have also ignored or assigned little importance to private sector debt because they contend that for every borrower there is a lender, and if you add those two totals together, then debt nets to zero – and thus its aggregate effect is neutral. They maintain that high levels of debt are not a problem because it all balances out.

That logic helps explain why those economists missed the mountainous ascent of US mortgage debt that caused the 2008 crisis, a total that rose from $5 to $10 trillion in five years. The profession's myopia relative to the 2008 crisis is now legendary, but, despite this, little has changed within orthodox economics, which continues to relegate private debt to a minor consideration.

These economists are correct on one point, however: when you consider borrowers and lenders, total debt does indeed net to zero. In fact, as we will revisit, financial assets equal financial liabilities, a well-established principle of economics, since the creation of an equal asset and liability results from the same transaction. In the case of a $1 million loan, a $1 million asset is created on the books of the bank, and a $1 million liability is simultaneously created on the books of the borrower. But although it nets to zero, private debt's effect is anything but neutral, and would only *be* neutral if lenders and borrowers were the same. But lenders and borrowers are decidedly not the same, and the distribution of these debts among actual borrowers and lenders matters greatly. Private debt borrowers are a broad swath of millions of individuals and businesses, including millions of small businesses; in contrast, lenders are much more concentrated, with banks alone accounting for 33 percent of all private sector debt.

Rising debt, after the proceeds have been spent, brings the obligation to pay interest and principal that directly reduces the spending and investing of the typical borrower. However, since private sector lending is concentrated in large financial institutions and wealthy individuals, the receipt of interest payments from borrowers does not commensurately increase their spending and investing. A significant number of those lenders are already spending and investing everything they intend to, and will most likely save rather than spend much of their increased earnings from higher lending levels. To use an economist's terminology, they have a lower marginal propensity to consume.

In other words, debt, once it reaches high levels, reduces the spending and investing of borrowers without commensurately increasing the spending and investing of lenders. This is a major reason why the effects and impact of rising debt are so uneven, and so important to study.

In fact, average-to-lower-income individuals have borne the disproportionate brunt of rapid debt growth, as is clearly shown in the proportion- ately greater rise of their debt in relation to their income and net worth. As such, rising debt has been a key element of rising inequality, which in the United States has increased markedly from a Gini coefficient of 0.40 in 1980 to 0.48 in 2019. The accumulation of debt is likely a consequence and a *symptom* of growing inequality, of course, because greater inequality means that more people have to borrow to make ends meet.

The data from the Federal Reserve's Survey of Consumer Finances indicates the trends. From 1989 to 2019, the debt of US households with net worth in the 1 to 59.9 percentile increased by 92 *percent* in ratio to their incomes. In stark contrast, households in the top 10 percentile saw debt to income rise by only *18 percent*.

For this bottom 59.9 percent, not only has their debt increased by 92 percent in relation to income, but their financial net worth (financial assets minus debt) has declined from 43 percent to 24 percent of their income. They have a diminished relative capacity to spend on education, investment, and other consumption. For the top 10 percent, it's a completely different story – in fact, almost the same story told in reverse. While their debt-to-income ratio has increased by only 18 percent, their financial net worth has *doubled* from 158 percent to 335 percent of their income. The contrast could hardly be more stark.

As part of this, since financial assets equal financial liabilities, then more debt, whether private sector or government debt, also means more assets – or wealth. Twice the debt to GDP does generally mean twice the financial wealth (assets) to GDP – but again it is the distribution of that debt and wealth that creates issues. As these numbers illustrate, the great preponderance of that asset growth has gone to the already well-off.

These numbers show the growing divide between average and wealthy Americans. And they show just as plainly how the accumulation of private sector debt exacerbates and widens that divide.

* * *

I've described the context and the problem: we have soaring private sector debt that strangles growth and widens inequality, and yet is largely ignored by mainstream economics. This book makes the case for a workable and meaningful solution. It is not another broadside against government spending or a call for austerity – far from it. We need to reduce the ratio of private sector debt to GDP, which is another way of saying reduce the burden of debt on households and businesses in relation to their income. It makes the case to unburden American households mired in debt with ideas that will improve lives, reduce inequality, and bring new vigor to the economy.

The proposals discussed in this book for certain types of broad debt restructuring and amnesty are intended to be politically feasible and thus to trailblaze a realistic path out of the debt trap. They target relief from the burden of mortgage debt, student debt, and more, along with an innovative and timely proposal for reducing government debt that is not dependent on austerity. These proposals are intended to be provocative but possible, and food for thought, even for those who disagree.

High Levels of Private Debt Stifle the Economy

We use the term "debt jubilee" to capture an ensemble of related ideas and terms that deal with broad debt restructuring, including forgiveness, cancellation, modification, or amnesty – terms that we will use somewhat interchangeably in this book. Debt jubilee takes many forms, as we will see.

To understand the importance of jubilee, we must understand three important realities about economies. This book will discuss these three realities in more detail because, once they are fully understood, the need for forms of jubilee, both big and small, becomes clearer:

- First, debt almost always outgrows GDP, and has reached very high levels in developed economies. It almost never grows at the same rate as (or a lesser rate than) GDP, reaching a sustained equilibrium. This debt growth is no accident, nor is it caused primarily by external circumstances; instead, it is an intrinsic, persistent feature of economic systems that comes from the very nature of growth and debt.
- Second, and as I've already begun to describe, high debt to GDP is harmful. It stultifies economic growth, brings financial distress to families, and widens inequality.
- Third, debt doesn't decline by itself, and it is

almost impossible to reduce it without significant, overt initiatives.

Some assume that debt reduction can easily be achieved, but as we will discuss in Chapter 3, it is very hard to accomplish and resists conventionally invoked solutions such as inflation and growth itself. In fact, none of the mechanisms, including inflation and growth, that are traditionally assumed to improve a county's debt profile work particularly well, if at all. Thus, the need – and case – for jubilee. To function at its best, our economy needs broad-based and inventive new initiatives for debt restructuring. Without these, debt levels will simply bring further growth challenges and burdens.

The good news is that jubilee would bring economic renewal. All would benefit: households would be financially stronger, and governments, businesses, and financial institutions would be better off *because* those households would be stronger.

Jubilee is not a quixotic, impractical dream of the soft hearted, but a key component of a well-functioning economy that should be integrated into that economy. It can improve the functioning of that economy – like the design features of an engine that prevent it from overheating and keep it running smoothly and optimally. Properly designed, jubilee would bring what has never been achieved in contemporary economic history: sustained growth coupled with a mitigation of the unchecked rise in the debt-to-GDP ratio and prevention of the crises that follow.

This is the future we should be aspiring to attain.

2

The Paradox of Debt

Jubilee would be an imperative solely based on the fact that private debt is so high. But jubilee is even more imperative because, as we have seen, not only is debt high in relation to GDP, but it is also growing ever higher – and presumably will continue to do so. But why is this so?

Before we answer that question, we must briefly ask: is private debt itself a problem? Economies cannot run without debt, after all, and the majority of this is private sector debt. As noted, the pervasiveness and necessity of debt have been evident since the earliest civilizations, which used credit systems to finance trade, agriculture, and more. The simplest acts in the earliest economies – someone buying something and committing to pay for it later, or providing labor and taking payment for it later – constituted the use of debt. These types of transactions permeate everyday commerce in essentially every society. Economic life as we know it would simply be impossible without enormous sums of private debt. It is intrinsic to the system. Twenty-first-century businesses such as supermarkets and retailers regularly use debt to meet their ongoing need to stock inventory. Manufacturers incur debt to buy raw materials to turn into finished goods. People use debt to purchase cars, houses, and other major assets.

So debt is neither intrinsically good nor bad. Debt is like water: indispensable, always there, and taken for granted and unnoticed except when there is dangerously too much or too little of it.

This is the paradox of debt. Debt growth brings economic growth, but too much of it impedes economic growth. Overly rapid private debt growth brings both boom and bust. And private debt growth leads to overload as it reaches perilously high levels and then plateaus, stifling growth. This is why debt jubilee is vital to the restoration of economic growth.

The Paradox of Debt

Why Debt Grows

It's not just debt itself but also its growth that is intrinsic; in other words, debt *growth* is built into the system. An economy could not operate without private debt, but it also could not grow without an *increase* in that debt. Debt is usually required to build new factories, create new products, or build housing developments. That's a major reason why debt always grows as fast as or faster than GDP: it takes debt to grow the GDP in the first place. Debt growth is not a coincidence, nor is it something that could be avoided in any economy where the participants aspire to grow. Without bank lending or government borrowing and spending, or both, GDP growth would be significantly constrained.

We can illustrate the necessity of debt for growth if we imagine an economy that has only ten people in it. One owns a supermarket, another owns apartments, another owns a bookstore, and so on. Each of them spends and also makes $50,000 each year. Thus, the GDP of the total economy is $500,000. No one starts with any savings.

If Person #1 wants to spend more on food, that person could only do that by spending exactly that amount less on something else: for example, books. In that case, GDP for this economy would stay at

$500,000. For the ten-person economy to grow, new money must be created.

One way to create that new money – in fact, the primary way in contemporary economies – is through borrowing. All new money is created with the simultaneous creation of a new liability, usually in the form of debt with a maturity and interest rate. Person #1 could borrow the money for the extra food, either from a bank or in the form of credit extended by the supermarket. In either case, debt supplies the extra money to grow the economy. That new money would be matched by and would provide the incentive for the production of additional food; thus, the economy would have both more money and more production.

Let's say Person #1 borrows $5,000 to buy more food. Because she borrowed the money for the food, she doesn't need to reduce her spending in some other area. In that case, GDP has increased to $505,000. It's that straightforward. The new money created is a financial asset that is matched by the newly created debt in the form of Person #1's loan.

The causes of growth that economists often cite, such as "increased net production" or "increased velocity," all require new money in the form of debt.

Our ten-person economy also shows, conversely, why a net contraction of debt shrinks an economy. If the next year Person #1 has to pay back her $5,000 food loan in full, then she will have to reduce spending to make that payment. She makes $50,000 but she will have to pay $5,000 on the loan, which means she only has $45,000 left to spend on goods and services that year. Assuming that the other nine citizens in our ten-person economy spend their full $50,000, the total GDP in this economy will now only be $495,000.

Ouch.

As we will discuss in Chapter 3, the contraction from net loan paydown was a key factor in the economic contraction of the Great Depression.

Even if we had a magic wand and could suddenly – expelliarmus! – reduce all private sector debt by some significant amount once debt levels got too high, the debt would recur; private sector debt and the ratio of that debt to GDP would climb again, since economic growth itself depends on debt growth, intrinsically. This is a key and often overlooked or misunderstood reality in policymaking.

As noted in Chapter 1, orthodox economists have ignored the problem of private debt partly because of declining rates, and also the belief that lending equals borrowing and therefore has a neutral impact. But one additional reason why they have ignored it is the deeply embedded assumption that financial trends are self-correcting and financial markets will always act through some inherent mechanism – perhaps an invisible hand? – to restore balance. This assumption holds that if some economic factor gets out of whack, the market will exercise its corrective discipline and soon enough that factor will return to within its previous bounds.

But private debt trends generally do not self-correct. The forces that bring debt growth are intrinsic rather than external and the upward debt march continues.

A careful study of the largest countries over the past 200 years shows that the ratio rarely even partially self-corrects – and then only as a result of a financial crisis or another disaster . . . before reverting to the same adverse trend.

This is shown clearly by the historical path for US private sector debt. In 1945, the private debt-to-GDP ratio stood at 37 percent of GDP, so low that economists hardly had cause or occasion to even notice the issue. But from there debt marched in an unbroken, non-self-correcting line all the way to 124 percent of GDP in 1990. Part of the reason for this was the massive real estate debt boom in the 1980s, which brought a banking and savings and loan crisis – a bust that brought the ratio down modestly to 118 percent of GDP by 1992. After that, the upward march resumed relentlessly and peaked at 168 percent, causing the 2008 global crisis. It tumultuously "self-corrected" after that crisis from that extraordinary peak down to 148 percent – but that was still above where it had been as recently as 2002. And then began to percolate upward again and stood at 164 percent at the end of 2020. (Since the early 1980s, this climb has been complemented by a similarly vigorous upward march of the government debt-to-GDP ratio, a phenomenon we will address in Chapter 5.) So, we see a seventy-five-year upward march in private debt from 37 percent to 164 percent, with two modest "deleveragings" (relative reductions in that debt) brought on by two painful banking crises. Balance has not been restored, and we have paid for our obliviousness to the debt burden over the decades with those two crises and the residual pileup of debt that now burdens growth.

The trends show that debt, being intrinsic to modern economies, doesn't self-correct to low levels.

New Money Is Created by Debt

As illustrated by our ten-person economy, economic growth requires new money and, essentially, all new money is created *only* with the simultaneous creation of a new liability, usually in the form of debt with a maturity and interest rate. Money is widely defined as a generally accepted medium for exchange and the paying of debt. In the United States, the most broadly used measure of money, or the "money supply," is the Federal Reserve's M2, which is the US total of checking deposits, cash, savings deposits, certificates of deposit, and individual money market mutual fund balances. M2 currently stands at $20.3 trillion. Most money in the US economy is simply deposits, and we will use that term.

Three acts are broadly referred to as "creating money" because they are thought to add deposits to the economy. In the first act, banks create money when they make loans to businesses, individuals, and others. In the second, the government issues debt in the form of US Treasury securities, and spends the proceeds. In the third, the Federal Reserve buys Treasury securities from commercial banks in "open market operations," or OMO. These last two acts are the ones most often referred to in the popular press as "printing money."

Let's look at what truly happens in each of these three acts in the United States.

Bank Lending

Banks create money by lending. Let's say that Betty Smith borrows $1 million from Bank MNO. When Betty goes to Bank MNO to borrow $1 million for expenses, the bank gives the proceeds of that loan to Betty by making a deposit into her checking account. That deposit is new money, which is a liability of the bank. (See Appendix Chart A.)

Money, the deposit in Betty Smith's account, *has been created by debt*, the loan to Betty, which she can then spend into the economy. These bank loans are a huge source of new money, and banks are a huge part of the debt and growth story. To give a sense of the magnitude: from 1980 to 2019, bank lending grew by $10 trillion, creating commensurate deposits. In 2020 alone, that growth was $365 billion. When banks buy securities such as mortgage debt or corporate debt from the non-bank private sector, it is in essence lending and amounts to the same thing. The increase in mortgage securities, corporate bonds, and municipal securities held by banks from 1980 to 2019 totaled $3.5 trillion. In 2020 alone, the increase was $816 billion.

Treasury Debt Issuance

When the US Treasury issues new Treasury securities, the purpose of which is to pay for the expenses of government, and then spends the proceeds, this new Treasury debt creates an asset. This comes first as an asset of the Treasury in the form of the resulting proceeds now in its own "checking account" at the Federal Reserve. Then when it is spent, it is an asset of the person/company the government is paying in the form of the deposit in their checking account. In this example, let's name Betty Smith as the person being paid. The deposit into Betty's account is new money (an asset) that comes from the new Treasury debt (a liability), and brings an overall increase in deposits *if* the security ends up being owned by the Federal Reserve or a bank. (See Appendix Charts B along with the accompanying note.)

A sense for the relative magnitude of this can be seen from the increase of $3 trillion in US Treasury securities held by the Federal Reserve and banks from 1980 to 2019. In 2020 alone, due to the extraordinary circumstances of the Covid-19 crisis, this increase was an additional $3 trillion.

Fed Open Market Operations

In the third example, probably the one most often glossed as "printing money," the Federal Reserve, through its open market operations, buys Treasury securities from a given bank by adding to that bank's "reserve" account at the Federal Reserve. This does not create new deposits, as shown in Appendix Charts C and accompanying note. (See also the accompanying note on quantitative easing.) However, when the Fed buys mortgage bonds or other non-Treasury securities from the private sector, a practice that scaled up substantially during the 2008 financial crisis and has continued through the Covid-19 crisis, it does create new deposits. Total mortgage and other non-Treasury debt held by the Fed from 1980 to 2019 increased by $1.5 trillion from 1980 to 2019, and by $677 billion under the extraordinary circumstances of 2020.

The growth in deposits in the US economy has largely been a function of these three acts, which illustrate and underscore the interdependence of the creation of new money with the creation of new debt. Debt increases are therefore built into the system.

Understanding these dispels the popular notion that money can simply be "printed" or "printed out of thin air" in a way that is free and with no strings attached. In each of these three acts, the money comes with a liability, or debt. Total financial assets equal total financial liabilities, before and after the transactions. Everything balances.

Other Reasons Why Debt Grows

In addition to these three dynamics, a few other factors contribute to the continuous amassing of debt.

First, a substantial portion of debt is effectively non-amortizing or amortizes very slowly. A great deal of debt is for assets or companies where the debt is *intended* to be a fixed, ongoing component of the funding structure (even though that can sometimes work to the detriment of the company). Moreover, much debt is in long-term mortgages, which are very slow to amortize. In other cases, the borrower hopes to make principal repayment on the debt but effectively never does, and only gets mired more deeply in debt. The overall effect is that a substantial portion of debt simply stays in place over the long run.

Second, debt accrues interest that compounds. If debt is required for growth *and* accrues interest that compounds, then this condition alone all but ensures that it will grow faster than GDP. That's the power of compounding.

Third, lenders have a powerful financial incentive to increase lending – it's how they win, and increase their own salaries, bonuses, and market power. This means that there is always a constituency committed to accelerating the growth of loans, and this has been true since the earliest civilizations.

Fourth, owners of assets, whether those assets are buildings or companies, have a tendency to use increased leverage to extract more money from these assets over time. Let's say you own a building worth $10 million that you purchased with a $10 million loan. Perhaps, over time, the value of the building appreciates by $2 million, such that it is now worth $12 million. If you can persuade your lender based on that appreciation to increase the amount of your loan by $1 million to $11 million, then you can put that $1 million directly into your pocket. This sort of thing happens all the time. Remember, the bank wants to grow its loans since it makes more money that way, and because the value of the building has appreciated, it still deems itself well collateralized. Both you and the bank win. Or, let's say you own a $10 million building that you bought with $3 million of your own money and a $7 million loan, because that's all the bank was willing to lend you. If, over time, the lender gets more comfortable with both you and the quality of the building, then you may be able to increase your loan amount to $8 million and put $1 million back in your pocket, even if the building does not appreciate in value. Those two examples help illustrate in part why asset owners are motivated to increase the debt on assets they own, and this is a powerful factor in rising debt levels.

Finally, there is always a level of unrecognized bad or unproductive debt in an economy. Some call it zombie debt. In these cases, borrowers can't repay the principal or perhaps can't even pay the interest, except through an increased loan amount. The borrower is barely hanging on, and the zombie debt should probably be written down or have increased loss reserves allocated against it, but both the borrower and the lender (and in some cases the regulator) are anxious to avoid that write-down, so the loan stays in place.

Because all of these factors hold true, debt generally grows as fast as, if not faster than, GDP, with a few exceptions that we will explore in the next chapter. And this builds a powerful rationale for debt jubilee as an integral component – a necessary fixture – of a functioning economy.

The Paradox of Debt

Is There a Limit to Private Debt Growth?

There is a practical limit to how high the private debt ratio can go, and its existence underscores the need for jubilee. A country's private sector debt is simply the sum of the debt of its households and businesses, and there is clearly a limit on how high the debt ratio of an individual or a business can go. To take an extreme example, an individual earning $100,000 a year can't carry a $10,000,000 mortgage, even if the interest rate is zero, because she couldn't afford the monthly payment of the principal. A business with gross revenue of $1,000,000 a year couldn't carry a conventional commercial loan of $50,000,000 because it couldn't afford the monthly payment of the principal – even if the interest rate was zero. The limit on private sector debt means individuals and businesses can't take on more debt, and that manifests itself as a slowdown in the GDP growth of the economy.

Countries tend to have lower growth through time as their private debt reaches higher levels. It's difficult to calculate the specific point at which private sector debt, once its increase has plateaued, starts to noticeably drag down economic growth, and certainly lower rates affect that calculation, but we estimate that the ratio is now likely around

150 to 200 percent. The drag on the economy occurs gradually along the way but appears more fully manifest at 150 percent. As we have seen, the United States, at 164 percent at the end of 2020, is growing well below its postwar rate. Above 200 percent there is an even greater level of slowdown, and a greater risk of economic calamity.

Very few countries have private debt ratios that have reached above 250 percent, because the households and businesses in these countries face such a greater debt payment challenge at that level. These few countries, including Switzerland and Sweden, are smaller economies that all have colossal current account surpluses (of which a trade surplus is a key component), without which they could not carry this level of private debt without significant adverse consequences. We will look more deeply at the impact of trade surpluses on debt in the next chapter.

Below this level, among the largest countries, China and France are now piling on private debt at a rate that could take them to 250 percent. They would do well to recall the private debt paradox: growth in debt can boost economic growth, but as that private debt at those countries' businesses and households reaches excessive levels, it can stunt economic growth and even bring crisis.

Will the private debt-to-GDP ratio in any of these countries self-correct down to 150 percent or 125 percent or even 100 percent of GDP? Never – or, at least, not without either an enormous economic calamity *or* the type of debt reduction programs that I propose in this book. The belief that financial trends are self-correcting to restore a more benign level of debt to income is dangerously misleading. It will take overt action to meaningfully improve any of these levels.

* * *

This chapter has shown that debt growth is built into the system. It has also shown the paradox of debt – that it is both essential for growth and a force that can stunt growth – and that debt does not self-correct. The next chapter looks at some widely held beliefs on how debt can be reduced, and considers why they haven't worked – and won't. In doing so, it builds the case for jubilee.

3

Policy Solutions That Won't Work

We want to reduce the ratio of private sector debt to GDP – which is another way of saying that we want to reduce the burden of debt on households and businesses in relation to their income. People may think this is easy but it's actually very difficult to lower debt. High debt is a stubborn malady that resists cure, for all of the reasons described in the previous chapter. Certain solutions for high debt have been cited frequently, and in this chapter we'll briefly examine and gauge the merits of each. They are:

- growth, the idea that we can grow our way out of a debt burden;
- inflation, the idea that we can inflate our way out of a debt burden;
- mass private debt paydown;

- high net exports; and
- moderating debt growth to let the math work in our favor.

Growing Our Way out of Debt

The most popular of these five potential solutions is the proposition that we can grow our way out of debt, which is known as deleveraging. We've heard politicians and economists make this claim frequently, especially in relation to public debt, and it's a highly appealing idea, but a very uncommon one historically. While modest deleveraging some-times occurs, meaningful deleveraging to a level low enough to positively affect growth rates is truly rare.

The most often-cited example of a country "grow-ing out" of its high government debt is the United States after World War II. From 1950 to 1980, the US government debt-to-GDP ratio did indeed fall from 86 percent to 32 percent, but that was only possible because of a massive releveraging of the *private* sector, where private debt simultaneously vaulted from 56 percent to 101 percent of GDP. From 1950 to 1980, the dollar total of govern-ment debt did not decline at all; in fact, government debt grew by $650 billion. But private sector debt skyrocketed by $2.7 trillion, which powered $2.6 trillion in GDP growth. Without that private sector debt growth, GDP would not have grown nearly this amount, and the government debt *ratio* would have stayed stubbornly high. This was more a trade-off, best understood as the debt version of "out of one pocket and into the other." Without that massive private sector debt growth, the improvement in the government debt ratio would have been impossible.

The converse happens as well: private debt deleveraging generally only occurs when accompanied by massive public debt growth, the only difference being the particular pocket out of which the money is moved. For example, during Japan's financial crisis in the 1990s, the private debt-to-GDP ratio peaked at a massive 221 percent of GDP, and the country spent the next twenty years deleveraging all the way down to 154 percent (which, as an aside, was a major contributor to its stunted private sector growth). But during that exact same time span, its government debt soared from 95 percent of GDP to 233 percent. From 1994 to 2015, Japan's private sector debt actually contracted dramatically, from ¥1,094 to ¥818 trillion – a collapse of ¥276 trillion – and its GDP would have collapsed by a similar amount, except that government debt grew by ¥811 trillion (part of this was used to purchase financial assets), and so

GDP managed to grow slightly rather than plunge, and the total debt ratio climbed from 307 percent of GDP to 387 percent. Had it not been for government spending and the resulting debt growth, the Japanese economy would have contracted severely.

So if the public debt ratio declines, it's usually because the private debt ratio has grown, and if the private debt ratio declines, it's usually because the public debt ratio has grown. This sort of trade-off has happened often.

My team of analysts and researchers and I simply can't find many cases where both the public debt and private debt ratio simultaneously declined meaningfully enough to boost growth. Since 1950, in the top ten economies in the world, there have been *no* instances where private and public debt in relation to GDP have together declined at least 10 percent within five years. If we expand that to look at the top twenty, we can find only three instances: Saudi Arabia, circa 2012, because of its very high net export surplus from oil (we will discuss the impact of net exports shortly); the Netherlands, circa 2019, because of its high net export surplus in agricultural products, manufactured goods, and more; and Mexico, circa 1988, because of restructuring and very high inflation. That's a mere three instances among the top twenty countries in over seventy years. We can't grow our way out of debt because it takes debt to grow.

Inflating Our Way out of Debt

If we can't grow our way out of debt, then can we inflate our way out of it? It's routinely claimed that we can, and although deleveraging through inflation is rare in developed countries and is generally confined to less developed countries, it does sometimes work. (In this case, I'm using a conventional definition of "inflation": an increase in the prices of goods and services, as opposed to the inflation of asset prices for things such as buildings and companies.) With high inflation, especially where inflation exceeds the effective interest rate on debt, prices and incomes will grow faster than the principal balance of debt and thus improve the debt-to-income ratio.

Take Brazil from 1994 to 1996. Total debt went from 126 percent to 93 percent of GDP as a result of inflation that was an egregious 2,076 percent in 1994 and a still-high 16 percent in 1996. Or Indonesia from 1998 to 2010, where total debt to GDP fell from 135 percent to 55 percent, but inflation averaged 13 percent per year during that span. Or Mexico from 1995 to 2001, where total debt dropped from 93 percent to 63 percent of GDP, as inflation averaged 20 percent.

But high inflation or hyperinflation, put simply, is a cure worse than the disease. It devastates savings and erodes household wealth.

And there is no guarantee that it will even work. During the United States' one recent major bout with inflation, from 1973 to 1982, where inflation averaged 8.8 percent (primarily due to OPEC-induced hikes in oil prices), total debt levels actually *increased* from 128 percent to 136 percent of GDP.

Furthermore, central banks have shown over the last decade that they may not even know how to create inflation high enough to make a difference, although they have employed the methods widely thought to cause high inflation, including low rates and high money supply growth, coupled with the government's massive deficit spending. We have seen increasingly lower rates, higher money supply growth, and higher deficit spending for most of the last forty years, and inflation has declined markedly in that span. It would take inflation in the range of 5 to 10 percent or more for several years as compared to the recent 2 percent level to make any real progress in deleveraging. Given that the US Federal Reserve has struggled over recent years to maintain even its target of 2 percent inflation, what makes us think it can increase inflation to this range of 5 or 10 percent for several years (notwithstanding the temporary food inflation from Covid-19 supply disruption)?

Paying Our Way out of Debt

Of course, the most straightforward proposed solution for reducing aggregate debt is simply to have consumers and businesses pay it down.

But asking private sector borrowers to pay down debt *en masse* won't work, for two reasons. First, most of them simply can't. If they had the resources to pay debt down, then they wouldn't have incurred the debt in the first place. The second reason is more important and slightly less obvious: if consumers and businesses paid down debt *en masse*, then it would crush the economy. That's because the dollars used to pay debt down would largely be funded by a reduction in spending, as illustrated by our ten-person economy in the previous chapter. Consumers now have $16.6 trillion in debt. An aggregate paydown of 5 percent of that debt would total $830 billion, and that would almost certainly come from an $830 billion reduction in spending. Since GDP is a measure of spending, it would bring a 4 percent collapse in GDP. (Debt amnesty, unlike a mass debt paydown, is a way to reduce debt without contracting GDP, because individuals are not required to reduce spending to pay debt. In fact, it would likely instead have the effect of *increasing* spending because funds used to pay debt would now be available for spending.)

I would always encourage an individual or business to be responsible in paying down debt. It is only a mass paydown, a net paydown in the economy as a whole, that would contract the economy, and to devastating effect. What is reasonable for an individual leads to unintended, contractive consequences if many act in the same way. That's precisely what happened from 1930 to 1934 during the Great Depression, when banks forced repayment of loans and borrowers paid down loans by a calamitous 23 percent. This is a poorly understood and underreported aspect of this period. The long lines of customers pulling their deposits meant not only that banks could not extend new loans but also that they could not *renew* loans even to their good customers. Where possible, it also caused them to call in the outstanding loans of good customers prior to maturity. For example, many banks did not renew mortgages, which had a typical maturity of five years, and so customers whose loans were maturing had to try to sell at the very moment when housing demand was collapsing.

Banks also had to call in the loans of many good businesses, such as retailers, that used bank loans to buy new inventory. Without those inventory loans, hundreds of thousands of otherwise good businesses failed. Loan balances collapsed nationally, with loans outstanding dropping from $111 billion in 1930 to $86 billion in 1934. That was a major contributor to why GDP, which had already started to drop, imploded – a full 45 percent drop (see Chart 7). The Federal Reserve or the Treasury could have stepped in much more assertively to provide the funding to prop up banks and prevent this, but didn't.

That inaction and the resulting contraction are at the heart and soul of why the Great Depression was so destructive. Contrast that to the 2008 crisis, when the Fed and Treasury did act to support these banks and prevent almost all the bank runs. As a result, private loan paydowns and the GDP decline were a comparatively small 4 percent and 2 percent, respectively.

Mass net paydowns, whether voluntary or forced, result in mass GDP contraction. And this is why they won't work to resolve the burden of debt. It is the equivalent of destroying the village – or the economy – to try to save it.

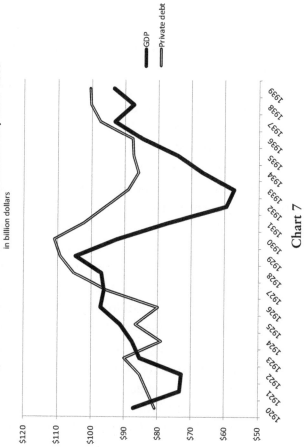

Depression Contraction: US GDP and Private Debt, 1920–1939
in billion dollars

GDP

Private debt

$120
$110
$100
$90
$80
$70
$60
$50

1920 1921 1922 1923 1924 1925 1926 1927 1928 1929 1930 1931 1932 1933 1934 1935 1936 1937 1938 1939

Chart 7

Policy Solutions That Won't Work

Exporting Our Way out of Debt

So we can't grow our way out of the high private debt problem, we can't inflate our way out of it, and we can't pay it down. What about debt reduction through high net exports? Unlike the first three options, this pathway actually does lead to national private debt reduction, and does work.

China is a great example. Its net exports (exports minus imports)-to-GDP ratio was 2.5 percent in 2002. Then the West went on its now infamous early twenty-first-century private debt binge, which enabled its private sector to buy more and more from China, and from 2004 to 2008 China's net exports exploded for a short time to as high as 9 percent of GDP. Consequently, its total debt-to-GDP ratio improved from 150 percent to 139 percent even while it posted strong GDP growth. Exports brought revenues to China's businesses that were not dependent on in-country sales, and therefore did not cause its domestic debt to grow. But that debt binge brought the crisis of 2008 to the West, and since the West could no longer buy as much as it moved from a debt binge into the purge of a recession, China's net exports soon collapsed to roughly 2 to 3 percent of GDP, and then to 1 percent in 2019, and its total debt has since unhappily catapulted to 260 percent of GDP, in part to compensate for this relative decline in exports.

Germany is another huge net exporter. Its net exports were modest until 2002, when it fully entered the EU's Economic and Monetary Union. Since then, its annual net exports have averaged an extraordinarily high 5.9 percent of GDP and in that time its public debt ratio has been flat and its private debt ratio to GDP has declined from 131 percent to 114 percent. Again, exports brought revenues that were not dependent on in-country sales, and therefore did not cause its domestic debt to grow. Germany achieved this high net export result partly because it entered the EU on favorable currency exchange terms, but its high net export gain is other EU countries' high net import pain. If history is any indication, Germany may be hard pressed to sustain this over the longer term because its neighbors may not be willing to tolerate the continued imbalance. If trade bonds ever fray, then Germany is notably vulnerable to a trade war.

Be that as it may, if the United States could just manage an export surplus of 5 to 10 percent of GDP for a decade or so, it would work wonders for its debt ratio and its economy. It could grow – perhaps even swell – GDP without growing debt, because that growth would come from those high exports.

But history does not suggest that the United States will be able to do this. First of all, it never has. For the last century, excepting the period of World War II and its immediate aftermath, there has been only one instance of an export surplus of more than 1 percent of GDP, and that was in 1964. Since 1975, there has not been a surplus at all, and in that time the US trade *deficit* has reached as high as 5.6 percent. It's a delusion to think that this could easily be turned around. President Trump tried hard, and the trade deficit only worsened during his presidency.

Second, if the United States was a large net exporter, then by definition other countries would have to be large net importers – and they would not be that pleased about it. Individuals and businesses in other countries that import from the United States would largely have to incur their own increase in debt to do so. And those countries' businesses that compete against the imported US products would not be politically passive. Countries that slip into a high net trade deficit eventually fight back – and it can lead to acrimony, finger-pointing, trade disputes, and trade wars. High export surpluses are difficult to sustain. Sure, improving the US export position would be a welcome way to improve its debt position, and I strongly encourage its efforts to do so, but it's unlikely that it will ever be a meaningful or primary path to deleveraging for the country. And, in any case, common sense and logic dictate that not every country in the world can be a net exporter, so this is an inherently limited solution.

Moderating Our Way out of Debt

There is one other way to reduce a country's total debt ratio, and it's an important technical note, even though it has rarely happened in any of the top twenty countries. We could simply *not let debt outgrow GDP by too much*. If a given country's total debt ratio is above 100 percent, especially if it is far above that figure, and it doesn't let debt growth wildly exceed GDP growth, then the mathematical ratio will improve.

For example, the UK's total debt ratio declined from 265 percent in 2012 to (a still high) 241 percent in 2019, even though its total debt outgrew GDP by £382 billion, or 68 percent. However, even this moderation has not been without consequence, as regulators have caused banks to deleverage and de-risk their balance sheets, driving marginal borrowers out of the market. At the same time, the

Bank of England's quantitative easing and other interventions have driven up house prices, forcing many younger people out of the market for mortgages. Nonetheless, the UK example does illustrate that even modest debt restraint in a high-debt country improves the ratio.

The important qualification to note, however, is that in the world's largest economies, debt is not outgrowing GDP by just a little bit, but by a whole lot. In the United States from 2014 to 2019, debt growth was 290 percent of GDP; in other words, almost three times higher than GDP growth. In China, debt growth was 333 percent of GDP; in Japan, 523 percent; and in France, 541 percent. Germany has not relied as heavily on debt growth because of its huge net export advantage, but nevertheless debt still outgrew GDP in this period by 125 percent.

(Note that such high ratios mean that these countries are not getting a full complement of GDP growth for their debt growth. This is what economists refer to as a deterioration in their credit intensity, and it's an undesirable trend.)

So it would take extraordinary, GDP-crimping restraint in debt growth by a given country and its private sector for this path to work. In our forty-seven-country database, with data from more than fifty years, we can find only five examples where this has been the primary path to an improved total debt ratio (as opposed to inflation or high net exports). Countries are rarely this disciplined. In fact, even if a given country with a 300 percent debt-to-GDP ratio held nominal debt growth to twice GDP growth, it could still take a decade to get even a 10 percent improvement in this ratio.

Nevertheless, debt ratios are so high for some developed countries that I would actually expect this "let math improve the ratio" factor to increasingly play at least some part in private debt reduction. But even with the improvement in these cases, the ratio would still be stifling.

* * *

We have established that our high level of private debt is a problem, and we've examined growth, high inflation, and private debt paydown as ways of reducing that debt ratio that are regularly invoked, only to find they are unrealistic or harmful. We have also examined approaches that *do* work, namely trade surpluses and a much greater restraint in the growth of debt, and we've applauded them. But we have been realistic about their limitations and seen that in the United States they cannot reasonably be expected to provide sufficient relief. Debt does not easily go down on its own, without some external and overt effort or policy action. So we need something else, and by process of elimination that something else is debt jubilee.

4

The Path to Private Debt Jubilee

With high debt in major economies, and with the likelihood that this will get worse rather than better, forms of debt amnesty are rapidly becoming must-haves rather than merely nice-to-haves. In other words, the imperative for debt amnesty is not the bleating of the unduly compassionate, but a hard-nosed assessment of the needs of the overall system. Productive, realistic forms of debt amnesty are necessary to maintain a well-functioning economy. As mentioned earlier, jubilee can be compared to the design features of an engine that keep it from overheating. If they aren't there, then woe betide us. And, in fact, woe often has.

The Path to Private Debt Jubilee

How Debt Restructuring Works – and Why We Need It

The widespread existence of debt forgiveness in antiquity profoundly attests to the universality and persistence of the debt accumulation issue. We need modern-day private debt restructuring and amnesty as a component of our economic system if we are to reduce an accumulated level of debt sufficiently to significantly improve things, and to do so without damaging the economy.

Debt restructuring is a modification of the terms of a loan that deals realistically with a borrower's ability to pay in times of distress. Typically, the lender reduces the principal balance or the interest rate, or extends the term of the loan. Debt restructuring already occurs routinely at individual lending institutions. Most have individuals or departments dedicated entirely to this type of effort, who work each day to reduce the principal or modify the terms of a given loan based on the borrower's distress. This happens often for struggling businesses, where, for example, a decline in market prices for a business' products means that it will not be able to make payments on its loan, and so the lender will sometimes extend the maturity of the loan, reduce required payments, and reduce the principal balance owed – sometimes in exchange for equity in the business. In fact, the largest corporate borrowers often have the most leverage to secure this kind of restructuring. As the oil tycoon J. Paul Getty once said, "If you owe the bank $100 that's your problem. If you owe the bank $100 million, that's the bank's problem."

Restructuring can also be employed for an individual if, after a job loss or medical emergency, the loan balance owed is far larger than the borrower's resources, and many creditors are pursuing repayment from that borrower. In this case, a given lender might "settle" for partial repayment since it believes the alternative might be no repayment at all.

However, to meaningfully impact debt numbers overall, jubilee needs to be implemented on a much larger scale than currently exists.

When I was a young banker, the head of the debt restructuring department in my bank pulled me aside and told me sternly that "the thing to do with delinquent debtors is throw them in jail." He said that for effect, but it brings to mind an issue and practice that dates back thousands of years. In spite of the legacy of debtors' prisons – Charles Dickens' father was once incarcerated in the infamous Marshalsea prison for failure to pay a small debt of £40 to a baker – and even debt enslavement, I must underscore that debt is a contract, and the payment of debt is a civil, not a criminal, matter. If someone finds that they cannot repay a debt because of a health crisis, job loss, or business failure, it is not a moral or criminal failing. As the late, brilliant anthropologist David Graeber reminded us: debt is a contract and contracts get modified all the time. The point of charging interest is partly to recognize risk, which implies that every act of lending is by its nature risky and therefore creditors can hardly be surprised when the risk doesn't pay off, or not to the extent that they'd hoped.

A growing list of politicians and economists have been advocating various large-scale forms of debt restructuring, and the Covid-19 pandemic has only amplified their message. (While this book focuses on the United States, the prospects for debt jubilee in developing nations, which fall beyond the scope of this book, deserve their own extensive treatment.) Economists Steve Keen and Michael Hudson have made broad proposals for debt jubilee, and presidential candidate Bernie Sanders called for outright forgiveness of all student debt. There have also been calls, especially in the immediate aftermath of the Great Recession of 2008, for mortgage debt relief and greater latitude to modify mortgages from such economists as Joseph Stiglitz and Mark Zandi.

Astra Taylor of the Debt Collective has written that any American president, should they desire, could make every penny of federal student debt disappear without consultation or negotiation because Congress granted the Department of Education legal authority in 1965 to extinguish federal student loan debt with an action called "compromise and settlement." She notes that canceling student debt would be a boon to debtors and the wider economy.

Laudably, the current administration may bring forward some form of a student debt relief program, a possibility that is highly encouraging.

I applaud these efforts and this advocacy. But these recommendations have not been fully embraced, and have engendered uneasiness and opposition based on three main objections: fairness, cost, and the moral hazard that debt forgiveness might create.

Is Debt Amnesty Fair? Too Costly? Morally Hazardous?

Fairness is a major, and serious, objection that demands consideration: how can we forgive one person's student debt, for example, when another person in a similar timeframe and in similar circumstances has fully paid theirs? For mortgages, consider the case of two neighbors, both with $240,000 homes, where one has a $300,000 mortgage because he bought at the height of the 2006 boom, and is thus $60,000 underwater, while the other has a $150,000 mortgage because she didn't. How can we justify forgiving $60,000 of that first person's mortgage, and not do as much for the second person? And how can this mortgage forgiveness be fair to renters, since they don't get a dime out of the program?

The Tea Party, which became influential in the aftermath of the 2008 financial crisis, emerged out of these types of protests against the perceived unfairness of the Obama administration's $75 billion proposal to reduce the monthly payments of nine million homeowners who were facing foreclosure. One ranting reporter on CNBC memorably questioned why he should be required to subsidize the mortgage of someone who had "made a mistake": that is, who had bought a house with the full knowledge that they did not have the resources to do so, but believing that they could profitably "flip" it.

Because of this fairness issue, some feel that the only approach to jubilee is simply to give a check to everyone, along the lines of the $1,200 pandemic-related checks issued as part of the 2020 CARES Act and the $1,400 payments included in the 2021 American Rescue Plan Act – but mandating that the money be used to pay down debt. I endorse support like this during crises such as the pandemic. However, unless we give a much larger amount to everyone – for example, $10,000 to $20,000, which would mean a multi-trillion-dollar expense beyond what has already been given during the pandemic – it is not going to meaningfully dent the student or mortgage debt problem, where the average debt amount is high, at $35,000 and $202,000, respectively. A more targeted approach, as proposed below, could have resulted in more relief for a lower cost and where most acutely needed. CARES-type checks, helpful and important though they may be, leave the debt problem largely intact.

The second objection to jubilee is the high cost, and the related question of who pays that cost. If mortgage lenders were asked to restructure all loans to fair market value and thus forgive a portion of the debt, those lenders would bear the direct cost of debt forgiveness. In the aftermath of the Great Recession, when this restructuring was most needed, there were so many troubled loans that forgiving them would have caused many lenders to fail. But if instead the government steps in, then many would reasonably ask why the *taxpayer* should bear this cost – which could run to tens or hundreds of billions of dollars or more. Even those who note that the government has the capacity to take this step may still justifiably question why funds should go to this program and not others.

The third objection is moral hazard. If someone gets bailed out of debt when they struggle, then won't that make them less prudent in their future borrowing habits, convinced that they will get bailed out again?

To get legislation enacted, jubilee programs need to take into account these objections, even if they do not fully address them. Their sponsors must take into account the "Overton window": the range of policies politically acceptable to the mainstream at any given moment.

Each of the programs here attempts to describe what is possible, rather than ideals of debt relief that are never likely to be politically embraced, with legislation that would be effectively "dead on arrival" at the steps of Congress. However, the downside of policy circumscription is more than offset by the upside of policy feasibility. These programs may strike some readers as too ambitious and other readers as too limited, but in either case, I aspire not to make the perfect the enemy of the good.

The Path to Private Debt Jubilee

Taken together, the programs described in this chapter, although benefits would be realized at different points in time, could bring the household debt-to-GDP ratio down to a level not seen in over twenty years, which would be a phenomenal, unprecedented post-World War II achievement for a developed economy.

In my view, the areas of private debt most in need of relief, and achievable, are student loans, mortgage debt, healthcare debt, and small business loans. These areas of excess debt disproportionately impact the economy, since they are among the largest components of private debt (as compared to smaller components such as credit card debt – see Chart 8). I'd love to see at least some program for other areas of household debt, but the areas listed are the most pressing. Here, I'll also touch on policies to reform bankruptcy, which is a crucial kind of jubilee that already exists, but could be improved.

Certain types of debt jubilees are best thought of as one-time – in other words, enacted for a short, specific period. Others can and should be built-in and become part of the system. Since debt is ever-accumulating, some forms of jubilee need to be ongoing, or we haven't really addressed the structural issue. For example, the two mortgage relief programs described below are likely best deployed

Chart 8

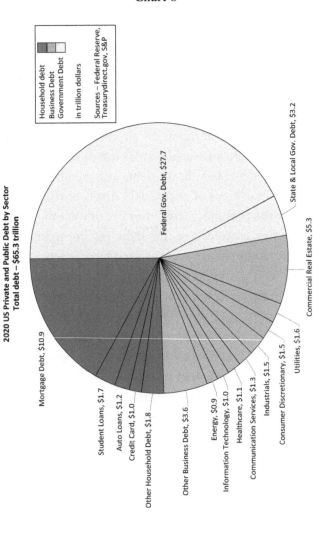

2020 US Private and Public Debt by Sector
Total debt – $65.3 trillion

Household debt
Business Debt
Government Debt

in trillion dollars

Sources – Federal Reserve, Treasurydirect.gov, S&P

Federal Gov. Debt, $27.7

State & Local Gov. Debt, $3.2

Commercial Real Estate, $5.3

Utilities, $1.6

Consumer Discretionary, $1.5

Industrials, $1.5

Communication Services, $1.3

Healthcare, $1.1

Information Technology, $1.0

Energy, $0.9

Other Business Debt, $3.6

Other Household Debt, $1.8

Credit Card, $1.0

Auto Loans, $1.2

Student Loans, $1.7

Mortgage Debt, $10.9

only as one-time or as-needed programs. The first would have been powerful if it had been enacted for a discrete period right after the 2008 banking crisis, and it is less acutely needed today because of a decade's worth of household mortgage refinancings at ever-lower rates. However, it may very well be needed for a future crisis, and the second can be used in today's Covid crisis. The student debt relief program, on the other hand, could become a permanent program. Bankruptcy reform is another example of a structural, ongoing form of debt amnesty. These programs are critical if we are committed to crafting an economy not prone to stultifying private debt levels and crisis.

Student Debt Relief

Student debt weighs like a millstone around the necks of millions of Americans for years after they have left college, deferring home buying, delaying household formation, and more.

I've visited extensively across the United States over the past few years to interview individuals and families about their financial lives and have been stunned to discover the pervasiveness of the student debt problem. There are forty-five million student loans outstanding in the United States and it seemed to me that in almost every family I encountered, one or more members of the extended family, and borrowers of every age, were struggling with student debt. I met a large number of parents who were still making payments on their own student loans while also co-signers on their children's student loans.

Student loan totals grimly skyrocketed to $1.7 trillion, or 8 percent of GDP, in 2020, up from $1 trillion, or 6 percent of GDP, in 2012, propelled by the rising cost of education and the proliferation of for-profit colleges of questionable value. As recently as 2003, student loans totaled a much smaller $250 billion, or 2 percent of GDP. Over the course of a decade, the proposal that I describe below (coupled with tighter prohibitions on loans for for-profit colleges without adequate achievements in graduation and job placement rates) could bring that number back closer to the 2012 ratio, with a goal of loans totaling $200 billion to $400 billion forgiven or on their way to being forgiven. This would bring us back to the ratio of student debt to income that existed before the recent, accelerated student debt explosion, which should be our policy objective and aim.

Conveniently, there is an existing program of student debt forgiveness for students who choose careers in the public or not-for-profit sector that could be modified and expanded: the Public Service Loan Forgiveness program. In this program, students who serve in the public or not-for-profit sector and also make 120 consecutive payments on their debt can have the remainder of that debt forgiven. Unfortunately, the government has taken a very narrow, seemingly obstructionist view of this program and has disqualified many participants for minor infractions, even after they had spent years believing that they were on track for debt relief. Thus an appallingly meager number of borrowers have benefited from this program, and many who have tried to take advantage of it have viewed the experience as a nightmare.

Nevertheless, we do have this precedent. Additional models for tuition assistance and debt relief programs have come with military and Peace Corps service. We can take these precedents and introduce a new voluntary program that expands and embraces forgiveness outside of the not-for-profit sector, if participants do substantial volunteer work for a qualified not-for-profit institution. I propose that if a student debt holder outside of the not-for-profit sector has made payments for ninety consecutive months, and has also done volunteer community service for an approved government or not-for-profit organization for 800 hours, then the remaining balance of that student's loan would be forgiven. The total hours of community service required could certainly be refined, or perhaps lowered to increase the program's feasibility. The details of the volunteer commitment in total hours are less important than the basic scaffolding of the program. I would shorten the existing public sector worker program from 120 months to 90 months as well, to make it much more achievable.

If the lender holding that loan is from the private sector, the government would then buy that loan and forgive it.

This policy approach addresses the fairness issue by requiring a commitment from the borrower to make a meaningful, sustained contribution not only of their payments but also of their time and labor in civic or charitable work.

For most, this would be a reduction in the amount they would pay, even taking into account their charitable labor. But it is one important step removed from universal student debt forgiveness. In effect it is an intermediate step between the current system, which crushes borrowers, and a full-fledged student debt jubilee. It's the option of an in-kind paydown of the loan.

An added benefit is that this option of community

service could help foment a wave of volunteerism, a renewed era of community service awareness and spirit that comes from doing purposeful civic work. Our objective should be to encourage participation in this program and facilitate it with coaching, counseling, and volunteer placement in order to achieve high levels of debt relief.

Proposals to provide debt relief to students have been described as regressive, with some justification. But it clearly touches the average American family and is a crucial and indispensable path toward improved financial lives for both working Americans and disadvantaged families. In that spirit, we should emphasize and orient these programs toward trades and technical schools as much as conventional universities (keeping in mind that nearly 40 percent of student debtors do not finish college).

And we should offer highly favorable interest rates and also make sure through clear lender disclosure that students who borrow truly understand the real and full costs of their education, once interest or other expenses are taken into account.

The question of fairness inescapably and forcibly shapes the policy environment around student loans, such that any pragmatic policymaker must balance the ideal against the practical, and take into account how a broad variety of Americans – those with and without student loans; those with and without college degrees – would react to any jubilee proposal.

Americans who did sacrifice to pay their debts or save and work to pay for college often have a deeply ingrained opposition to student debt relief, so let's explore this objection further. A November 2020 op-ed piece by Jeff Jacoby in the *Boston Globe* typifies the broader objection to across-the-board student debt forgiveness:

> One Iowa father's encounter [with a politician who is an advocate of across-the-board student debt forgiveness] captured the raw unfairness of the idea.
>
> "My daughter's getting out of school. I saved all my money [so] she doesn't have any student loans," the man said. "Am I going to get my money back [if the government forgives all student debt]?"
>
> "Of course not," [that advocate] answered.
>
> "So you're going to pay for people who didn't save any money, and those of us who did the right thing get screwed," said the father, visibly upset. "My buddy had fun, bought a car, went on vacations. I saved my money. He made more than I did, but I worked a double shift, worked extra. My daughter's worked since she was 10."

That exchange vividly illustrates the injustice of

student-debt proposals that would, in effect, punish those who saved and worked more to pay for college, those who deferred higher education until they could afford it, and those who responsibly repaid their loans – by forcing them to pay for those who didn't. Even more outrageous, it would compel the two-thirds of Americans who didn't earn a college degree to help pick up the tab for many of those who did. . . .

Democrats a year ago may have thought that offering a bailout to college-educated, upper-middle-class voters made political sense. But how can they still think so after an election in which the "blue wave" they expected never materialized, in part because of Republican gains among working-class Americans without college degrees?

Whether we are persuaded by this argument or not, it represents a widely held concern. If there is across-the-board forgiveness without provisions to address this issue of fairness, it will stoke deeper resentment in the United States.

Make no mistake – I am for student debt jubilee. It gives a boost to individuals and families for their financial advancement, and it also recognizes that education is critical to the continued evolution of the American economy, especially in a world where other nations, including China, have narrowed the gap with or surpassed the United States in higher education attainment.

The question, however, is whether the issues of fairness can be sufficiently addressed such that some form of jubilee legislation can be enacted. My belief that something needs to be done *soon* has turned me into a pragmatist on this and other programs proposed in this book. I would rather get some debt relief *now* than wait for a more comprehensive form that may never get enacted at all. I believe that could be accomplished with the addition of a community service requirement for the borrower.

Mortgage Debt Relief

In the aftermath of the Great Recession, home values plunged, and consequently over ten million of the nation's fifty-two million mortgages went underwater, meaning that the value of their home was at least 10 percent lower than the amount of their mortgage. This compares to fewer than three-and-a-half million mortgages today. Mortgage debt is by far the largest component of household debt (see Chart 8), and thus debt problems here are most likely to bring greater damage to the economy as a whole.

The Path to Private Debt Jubilee

Here's a possible program to forgive the underwater portion of owner-occupied mortgaged properties. Let's say you have a home with a $300,000 mortgage but the market value of the home is $240,000, such that the home is $60,000 underwater. If a lender were to write down the amount of that mortgage to the current market value of the home, they would normally have to take the entire $60,000 write-down as a loss at that moment. For this reason, lenders are loath to write down a mortgage, especially if the borrower is current on payments, even if they are struggling mightily and treading water to remain so.

I propose a program that would be voluntary for the borrower. It would allow a lender to write down the underwater portion of the mortgage over thirty years, instead of all at once, if that lender in turn immediately reduces the principal on the borrower's mortgage by that same amount, and also proportionally reduces the monthly payment. There is regulatory precedent for such deferrals. It would be done at the borrower's option. The lender would still be able to take the tax benefit of the loss in the current period, and the deferred amount would not be counted against capital or reserves.

In exchange for this benefit, the borrower would be required to give the lender some portion of the gain on the subsequent sale of the home, based on the amount forgiven. Let's say that gain portion is 30 percent. When the home is sold, the lender would get 30 percent of the gain. This feature would directly address the fairness issue: anyone willing to cede a portion of the gain on sale to the lender would qualify to participate.

This policy would be attractive to many lenders because they would get the full tax benefit of the loss but only have to write down one-thirtieth of the loss each year, and would also enjoy a gain on sale. This last component, which is in essence a debt-to-equity feature where a reduction in debt is exchanged for the gain of part ownership, enhances the policy's appeal. The debt-to-equity feature means that something is required of the borrower, which addresses the fairness issue. But its most attractive element for the lender would be thirty-year loss amortization, coupled with the current tax benefit.

The fact that mortgages are securitized complicates this solution, but that issue is not insurmountable and the legal and technical issues can be parsed out and addressed. For example, the securitization holder could be given the rights to exchange or sell these mortgages to a lender that could fully utilize the tax and other advantages.

If this program had been enacted in 2009, it would have provided significant relief to millions of homeowners and allowed many to remain in their homes. It could have been enacted for a limited period – for example, through 2012 – and only for mortgages of less than $500,000. After so many mortgage loan refinancings of the past decade, the program is less needed today, but would be a powerful tool in the economic toolbox that could bring substantial relief to many in a future crisis.

At this distance, it is easy now to overlook the profound and pervasive economic damage to working Americans wrought by mortgage problems. A number of commentators, including Trump's political advisor Steve Bannon, attributed much of Trump's success in the 2016 election to this economic wreckage. Banks got bailed out, but households didn't.

With this proposal, the overall mortgage loan market would have remained intact, but would have had a mechanism to handle the underwater mortgage problems that plagued the US economy for years after the 2008 crisis. The owner simply would have been given an additional choice: a lower payment today but less upside in the future, or the same higher payment today but full upside in the future. It would not impact future buyers, since that home would be sold at fair market value.

Our analysis finds that in the immediate aftermath of the 2008 crisis, more than $800 billion of the mortgage debt total was underwater. This proposed program, *if it had been fully enacted in these years immediately after the crisis*, could have reduced that underwater mortgage debt total by as much as that full amount, and certainly no less than half that amount. In 2000, before the boom, household mortgages were 47 percent of GDP and at the 2007 peak reached 74 percent of GDP. After a decade of write-downs and refinancings, that ratio has come down close to the 2000 level, and if this policy had been fully deployed before 2012, it could now be below that level.

We could do something in this same spirit today. We could use this same policy architecture to deal with mortgage issues wrought by the Covid-19 crisis, although underwater mortgages are not the specific problem this time around. Instead, mortgage payments deferred through Covid-19 relief regulations are going to have to be paid or otherwise dealt with at some point after those relief programs end. At that point, many borrowers with ongoing diminished financial circumstances due to the Covid-19 crisis will face a challenge even making current mortgage payments, to say nothing of covering those missed payments.

A program could be offered through the end of 2023 that would allow the missed payments and interest, *plus* up to an additional 20 percent of the principal balance, to be written down – all at the borrower's option. This would provide significantly lower payments and thus substantial relief to borrowers who take advantage of the program. It could be a "Covid-19 mortgage relief act" that could bring tens of billions of dollars of additional principal relief to those whose need is most acute. Again, the lender would amortize the write-down over thirty years, get a current tax benefit, and have negotiated equity upside upon sale. The borrower would see a reduced monthly payment, and the lender and borrower would have an effective way to deal with Covid-19 payment challenges. (Some lenders may already be giving borrowers the option of putting missed payments into a subordinate lien repayable only when they refinance, sell, or terminate their mortgage. The 20 percent reduction in principal that I'm proposing would be in addition to that relief.)

In any case, mortgage problems will perennially occupy a place at or near the top of the list of debt challenges in future debt crises for the simple reason that home mortgages constitute by far the largest category of private debt (followed by commercial real estate). Debt related to real estate has been the most significant and destructive factor in most major financial calamities – the United States in the late 1980s, Japan in the 1990s, the Great Depression of the 1930s, and many more – and so mortgage debt relief deserves our ongoing attention.

Healthcare Debt Relief

Healthcare debt has become a scourge. According to the Consumer Financial Protection Bureau, half of all overdue debt on credit reports in the United States is from medical debt.

Liz Hamel and her colleagues at the Kaiser Family Foundation have reported that 26 percent of adults in the United States between the ages of 18 and 64 disclosed they or someone in their household either had issues paying or were completely unable to pay medical bills in the last year. A survey reported on by Sara Collins and her colleagues at the Commonwealth Fund which represents 193.5 million US adults between the ages 19 and 64 found that 24 percent of them reported problems paying, or an inability to pay, medical bills in the prior year.

Among major economies, this is a distinctly American problem because of the United States unique – outlier – healthcare system. In my conversations with families across the nation about their financial lives, healthcare expense has been a consistent refrain and lament. From high monthly premiums to high deductibles, from unexpected healthcare problems to surprise medical bills, it is a nightmare for many.

Healthcare debt is not surprising. Millions of families are uninsured, and those that are insured increasingly have deductibles as high as $3,000 or $5,000. In a country where the Federal Reserve reports that four in ten adults would have difficulty covering an unexpected $400 expense, unplanned medical expenses and surprise medical bills can trigger a debt chain reaction that puts a household in arrears on credit cards, auto loans, student loans, mortgages, and other debt, trapping them in a blizzard of late fees and collector calls and adding unbearable stress to their lives. The issue is so acute that some simply postpone needed medical procedures, which compounds their future medical problems and increases future medical costs.

I propose a straightforward solution: a means-tested program whereby individuals with less than $85,000 in household income could apply for the government to reimburse them for any debt incurred for a select number of critical healthcare expenses, including select procedures for diabetes, cancer, and heart disease.

Healthcare debt totals are hard to quantify since they can appear in different loan categories: credit extended by hospitals, credit cards, bank installment loans, credit union loans, and more. Our best estimate is that total healthcare debt is in the range of $300 billion to $650 billion, and that this program could provide relief of $100 billion to $200 billion.

To an extent, this program addresses the fairness issue by being means tested, and the issue of moral hazard does not apply since no one chooses to get sick. It is also important to note that, in addition to bringing relief to households, it would bring significant relief to healthcare providers and lending institutions. It would also bring relief to the economy as a whole, since healthier citizens and diminished bad debt would be a boon for the entire system.

Legislation is most likely to be passed when there are benefits to all parties affected, or at least when no party is harmed, and this is true for all of the programs proposed in this book. Legislation is least probable when the objective is for one or more constituencies to lose.

Better yet, the government could introduce an overall catastrophic health insurance plan as part of an expanded healthcare initiative that would cover people for a select set of procedures, and reimburse them for deductibles. Of course, the single-payer plan that has been advocated by many would also solve this problem.

Bankruptcy Law Reform

We've sketched three powerful debt jubilees, of a kind. The mortgage debt relief program would be designed as a short-term dispensation, while the student debt and healthcare relief programs would be structural and ongoing. We should add to these policies some changes to and modifications of US bankruptcy laws that would also act as structural, embedded forms of debt amnesty. In one sense, an individual who files for Chapter 11 bankruptcy is getting a "jubilee" in the form of a debt reset, or clean slate, albeit with penalties to their credit rating and their subsequent access to credit.

As a long-time bank CEO and career lender, I saw Congress enact a number of changes to make these laws stricter, and I saw firsthand the impact on consumer credit losses that resulted. After careful analysis, I came to believe that stricter bankruptcy laws did not improve the consumer credit losses incurred by lenders as proponents of stricter laws had intended, and in fact may have exacerbated those losses because stricter laws made borrowers' struggles all the more difficult and damaging. Further, I now believe that, over the long haul, more thoughtful and less punitive bankruptcy laws, such as those described below, will lessen credit losses because they will result in financially healthier households.

Bankruptcy laws that provide balanced, appropriate relief also result in more careful, more prudent, and thus healthier lending practices. Bankruptcy is therefore not only a way to cope with calamity but also a check on the system, a safety valve that curbs excessive lending practices.

The introduction of bankruptcy measures to provide economic and societal relief from high debt has ample precedent. Historically, during a number of periods of national financial distress in both the United States and elsewhere, bankruptcy laws have been enacted to allow for increased debtor relief and to provide a more orderly basis for dealing with distressed debt. Some were intended as temporary measures and repealed after a few years. In the United States, these go back as far as the

Bankruptcy Acts of 1800 and 1841, occasioned by the financial crises of 1796 and 1837, respectively.

For years, the lending industry advocated for stricter bankruptcy laws, such as the Bankruptcy Abuse Prevention and Consumer Protection Act of 2005, on the argument that bankruptcy courts were full of irresponsible debtors who abused the system, even though the evidence strongly suggested that the bankruptcy system functioned well, was rarely abused, and did not require significant reform to address irresponsible debtors. Rather than frivolously abusing the system, the data showed that nearly 90 percent of families declare bankruptcy for one of three profound reasons, largely beyond their control: a job loss, a medical problem, or a family breakup.

Thoughtful bankruptcy reform should ensure that household borrowers can retain their jobs and keep their families together. It should be designed to repair rather than punish. Much of the constructive thinking in this area has been led by Senator Elizabeth Warren, and my recommendations reflect her work and ideas.

Appropriate bankruptcy reform would:

- allow people to modify their mortgages in bankruptcy, which is generally prohibited by law, since the restriction on mortgage modifications in bankruptcy, even though other types of debts can be renegotiated, often hurts both bankruptcy filers and mortgage lenders;

- allow renters in bankruptcy to continue paying their rent if this would avert eviction;
- release a debtor no longer in residence at a home from future liability for taxes and code violations;
- allow debtors to keep their cars by paying the lender the fair market value of the car over a reasonable time, thus making it easier for them to get to their jobs and care for their families;
- allow student loans to be discharged in bank-ruptcy, just like other consumer debts; and
- allow accumulated local fines and fees to be discharged.

These six reforms would put families on a firmer foundation for a new start, and get them to a place where they could pick up the pieces and rebuild their financial lives – all the more vital and reasonable when we remember that most entered bankruptcy because of an external crisis. Everyone benefits in the long term when financial lives are rebuilt.

Beyond these recommendations, smaller reforms could streamline paperwork and allow attorneys' fees to be paid over time, so as not to unduly drain these families' extremely limited resources. And there could be more stringent consequences for acts by creditors that are already prohibited, including attempting to collect discharged debts and debts during bankruptcy proceedings.

These bankruptcy reforms would benefit American households, the nation's household debt burden, and the health of financial institutions. That would translate into an economic benefit because it would hasten the return of families to economic vibrancy.

Although it is impossible to quantify, my own judgment is that, over time, these bankruptcy reforms could peel billions of dollars a year off the total of household debt.

Small Business Debt Relief

I view the debt of very small businesses as closer to personal debt than to that of major corporations, since it is most often the province of individual or family ownership, and so it deserves consideration for jubilee as well. Small businesses also deserve special consideration because they have borne the brunt of lockdown, shutdown, and limited-capacity policies at local and state levels during the Covid-19 crisis, even while behemoth chains have been the more *de facto* beneficiaries of relief policies. Small businesses feel the brunt of a generation of excessive, burdensome business debt.

I would propose a temporary and voluntary program of small business debt relief similar to the mortgage program proposed above. For loans where the enterprise or collateral value has fallen below the loan value, a lender could write down all or part of the difference, and over a span of thirty years, so long as they restructured that debt to reduce the principal to the borrower by that same amount.

In exchange, the borrower would give the lender a negotiated portion of the gain on any future sale of the business or its key assets. The lender could take the loss in the current year for tax purposes, and the deferred loss would not be counted against that lender in the calculation of capital and reserve adequacy.

The loan total for small businesses is hard to pin down since the definition of a "small business" varies. The Small Business Administration (SBA) defines it as a business with fewer than 500 employees; the Federal Deposit Insurance Corporation (FDIC) has called for a definition of "small business loans" as commercial loans of $1 million or less. Our estimate is that small business loans total $645 billion, and that the program described here could reduce that total by between $80 billion and $160 billion. This is a small total, comparatively, but I view most of this as household debt, essentially, and this would be crucial relief for those households, which is our primary concern in this book's debt relief proposals.

In addition to my proposal here, a tilt toward debtor relief in small business bankruptcy would be a game changer.

Moderating the Debt Bias in Tax Law

If our overall objective is to moderate the growth of private debt, then there is another structural opportunity to consider. US tax laws are currently biased toward the use of debt instead of equity. My recommendation would be to partially reverse that bias by modifying the tax treatment of debt and equity for large businesses.

There are two primary ways that companies raise money. The first is through debt (a loan or a bond), and the second is through equity (selling shares of the company). Corporations, if they use debt, receive a tax deduction for much of the interest they pay. If they raise equity and pay a dividend on that equity, then they don't get a favorable tax deduction for that dividend payment, while the recipient of that dividend does pay tax, giving rise to the complaint of double taxation.

Thus, the tax code itself creates at least some added incentive to use debt over equity, and is at least part of the reason why leverage increasingly gets used to finance acquisitions of assets and other companies. A change in the tax code with less favorable treatment of debt and more favorable treatment of equity could reduce this bias toward debt, though full interest deductions should be preserved for smaller businesses.

* * *

Jubilee programs for private sector debt such as the ones I've described here would curb its insidious upward climb and create a much-needed economic boost. I would welcome any and all other debt amnesty ideas. A cleaner debt slate frees households for the kind of increased spending and investment that drives an economy forward. But more fundamentally, it would profoundly transform the lives of Americans: they would have much higher hopes that they could afford their children's educations, keep their homes, and handle healthcare bills that otherwise overwhelm them.

The laws enacting each of these programs should ensure that debt forgiveness is not taxed.

Collectively, these programs, if enacted as described, could result in as much as $1.5 trillion in debt relief, primarily to households, with a household debt-to-GDP ratio as low as 65 percent, a level not seen in twenty-five years. These programs could mitigate or eradicate what amounts to the debt servitude of millions of Americans and would be a mammoth achievement for a twenty-first-century developed economy. With this, the private sector could more easily resume its role as a driver of growth and prosperity. Just as importantly, these programs would establish or improve mechanisms for built-in debt relief that would provide future, ongoing moderation of debt levels. With these, debt ratios could stay flat or further improve. Lastly, and crucially, they will help establish the precedent and principle of debt amnesty as a key, integral component of economies.

The problem, of course, extends to the other three of the world's major economic systems – China, Europe, and Japan – which together constitute the vast majority of the world's GDP and debt. Perhaps some of these ideas could apply to these economies as well, where the debt problem continues to grow. I have a sense that China may be increasingly employing forms of preemptive debt restructuring and recapitalization, based on the lessons learned, formative experiences gained, and hard-earned skills acquired from dealing with its 1999 debt crisis. But China is alone among these major economies in controlling all parts of the equation itself – the companies, the banks, and even the lives of its citizens – and therefore can quietly and preemptively enact forms of jubilee in a way that other countries would find vastly more difficult politically.

The Social and Economic Benefits of Jubilee

We've used the term "jubilee" in this book, and emphasized it in this chapter, because we think it captures the idea of reducing the heavy debt load of households and small businesses. But there is no question that jubilee is a provocative idea, so we have to consider not just the political feasibility but also its potential benefits for society and the economy. Why would any government want to establish debt relief? Here, twenty-first-century politicians and policymakers can learn from ancient civilizations and their rationales for debt amnesty.

Kings in these ancient civilizations had a number of reasons to call for debt relief. The king's mercy, as demonstrated through debt amnesty, secured allegiance to and admiration for him. In *Leviticus 17–22*, the modern Jewish scholar Jacob Milgrom describes the jubilee found in the Torah as "the priestly response to economic injustice."

But in the largest sense debt relief was – and still is – about the balance of power between the rich and poor. And, just as importantly, it was about the balance of power between the government and the wealthy, since ancient jubilees curbed the power of the wealthiest families. Lending in the earliest societies was often purely the province of the palace and temple, but over time powerful merchant and trading families increasingly made loans, and lending became one of their most profitable activities. Income from lending increased their wealth, and even lending defaults on land loans increased their wealth as they took over the land collateral and thus added to their massive landholdings. As their wealth accumulated, they became a threat to the king's power, purchasing their own networks of influence and even fielding their own armies. Commanding those families to forgive debt effectively curbed their wealth and checked their power.

The success of jubilee as a constraint on the power of the wealthy can be appreciated in hindsight if we consider what happened when debt amnesty *disappeared* in ancient societies. As the wealth of powerful families rose, their resistance to debt amnesty rose as well, and the practice gradually decayed. The resistance of creditor families to debt amnesty sometimes escalated into violence and civil war, with creditors pitted against kings who were trying to cancel debts and reverse the monopolization of land acquired through loan defaults. Creditors eventually got the upper hand. By the later years of the Roman Empire in the West and during the Ming Dynasty in China, large-scale debt amnesty had largely disappeared. The small borrower's security of property was displaced by the sanctity – and military enforcement – of debt contracts. In some respects, that transition defines modern civilization. Time went from being cyclical, with a return to beginnings, to linear, with the intention and hope of unbroken accumulation.

But with the disappearance of debt amnesty – the royal power to preserve widespread land tenure – came greater poverty, inequality, economic contraction, and even collapse. Some historians saw the discontinuance of debt amnesty as a factor in Rome's demise. Michael Hudson notes that Livy, Plutarch, and other Roman historians – and even the more recent historian Arnold Toynbee – blamed Rome's decline on the creditor land appropriation, and thus disenfranchisement, of the broad population. The famous conflict between Cicero and Catiline developed partly over the populist appeal of Catiline's debt forgiveness agenda and Cicero's opposition to the same as Cataline unsuccessfully advocated *tabulae novae*, the elimination of debt for all. "Barbarians had always stood at the gates," wrote Hudson, "but only as societies weakened internally [from this debt accumulation] were their invasions successful."

In ancient civilizations, the government would bear the cost of debt forgiveness on loans that it had made, and it could decree that losses from loan forgiveness on loans made by merchants and traders, or the "private sector" as we call it today, would be absorbed by those merchants and traders. But decreeing a loss to private sector lenders in the twenty-first century would be all but politically impossible, creating loss and risk for those institutions and provoking justified cries of unfairness, unless designed appropriately. To be palatable, this type of debt amnesty needs features that make it politically feasible and economically sustainable. For example, for the mortgage lending write-down to fair market value, I have proposed above that lenders be given thirty years to amortize the loss, coupled with the equity upside and the immediate tax write-off.

Ancient debt relief restored the balance of power between the government and wealthy families but it also preserved a population free from bondage and ready to serve in the king's army and to perform a fixed amount of labor for him. That might mean assigning to the king a portion of their crops or helping to build the magnificent public works of the era. Translating this rationale for jubilee into contemporary economies, debt relief frees households for economic activity and growth.

Finally, ancient civilizations understood that lending was necessary, and amnesty was in this sense a conservative act, because it preserved an indispensable lending function but prevented loans from strangling these economies. These civilizations also understood that debt relief is a recurring need. Debt, once relieved, builds up again, and so debt relief is best installed as a fixture of economic systems. Bankruptcy is an important form of this embedded relief, as is the student debt relief that I propose. Debt always grows, so its management is a permanent, ongoing challenge.

Debt amnesty was, and still is, as much about power – its preservation, distribution, and subversion – as altruism. It was also about the social and economic stability of the culture, a lesson that we can learn from ancient jubilee precedents.

The Path to Private Debt Jubilee

Turning to Government Debt Jubilee

Financial assets are conjoined with financial liabilities, and thus the cancellation of debt brings the simultaneous destruction of assets and wealth. In the twenty-first-century United States, that is tantamount to dooming any legislation offered unless it successfully deals with that issue. Our proposals address that issue for private sector debt by having the government assume the cost for student and healthcare debt, and by giving the private sector thirty years and an equity upside in the case of mortgage and small business debt. Which brings us to the next big question: how do we deal with that increased government cost and debt?

An idea not captured in ancient debt amnesties is the debt of the government itself as the beneficiary of the program – in essence, the government repudiating its own debt. Governments in these earliest civilizations essentially had no debt. That came later, and not without controversy. It would be inadvisable for the US government to repudiate its own debt today because most holders of government securities are not foreign governments but US citizens, through private holdings such as retirement funds, mutual funds, exchange traded funds, claims on payments from Social Security, and more. A debt jubilee for the government, in other words, would obliterate a significant portion of US household net worth. The next chapter considers ways that our government can ease or moderate the burden of its own debt, given the complicating factor of wealth destruction.

5

The Enigma of Government Debt

It is true that private debt forgiveness has a cost. There is no avoiding that. I would expect the cost to government of these proposed jubilee programs to be between $300 billion and $600 billion – high but manageable. But this would risk the very "one pocket into the other" conundrum we described earlier.

Federal government debt, though smaller than private sector debt, is much more closely scrutinized and hotly debated. So we need to start, as we did with private debt, with the question of whether high government debt is intrinsically a problem. It has long been assumed to be so, and politicians often reinforce that idea. President Barack Obama once lamented that America is relying on "a credit card from the Bank of China," though China's ownership of US debt is currently less than 5 percent of the total. And during the Great Recession, when a journalist asked him, "At what point do we run out of money?", he responded, "We are out of money now," although that was not remotely true.

The partial government shutdown in late 2018 and early 2019, during which 800,000 workers went unpaid, was based on the presumed pernicious effects of higher government spending and debt. This belief is widespread because a number of economists, including the authors of leading macroeconomic textbooks, such as Greg Mankiw, have long taught that high government deficits and debt will lead to high inflation, crowd out private investment, and even cause a run on the dollar, resulting in a financial crisis.

Since 1981, the US government has routinely posted large deficits and the government debt-to-GDP ratio has *almost quadrupled* – and none of those feared and predicted consequences have come to pass. Quite the contrary. During the almost forty-year explosion of US government debt from 1981 to 2020, price inflation has plummeted, not increased; interest rates have collapsed, not risen; and buyers for government debt have been ample to the task, as evidenced by those declining rates. Likewise, the Japanese government has posted recurring deficits and its debt has *almost quintupled* relative to GDP – and inflation has not materialized there, either.

These dire prognostications about the consequences of rising government debt in the United States haven't materialized for one simple reason: the US government has monetary sovereignty, which means that it issues and borrows in its own currency, a status it has fully held since it went off the gold standard in the early 1970s.

Welcome to the World of Monetary Sovereignty

So let's revisit exactly what happens when Treasury debt is issued. As discussed, when the Treasury borrows and then spends $1 million to pay government employees or to buy goods and services from the private sector, keeping in mind that the purpose of borrowing is to spend and the two events are essentially linked, two key things happen. (The two things also most often happen in a similar time frame.) First, although the government has become $1 million more indebted, the individuals or businesses that get paid become $1 million wealthier, as in the case of our hypothetical Betty Smith (see Appendix Chart B and accompanying note). Not a bad outcome, and in keeping with the Financial

Assets Equal Financial Liabilities principle. Second, if the Treasury security is bought by a bank, the total of bank reserves in the system (money that the banks can use to buy Treasury bonds, among other things) *remains the same and does not decrease*. The reserves of the bank that bought the security decrease but the reserves of Betty's bank increase by the same amount when the government pays her. The banking system has exactly as much capacity to buy more Treasury securities after the transaction as it did before. Similarly, if the Treasury security is bought by a non-bank dealer (or individual, or other private sector entity), then the total of bank deposits in the system remains the same and *does not decrease*. The deposits of the dealer that bought the security decrease but Betty's bank deposit increases by the same amount when she receives payment. The system has exactly as much in deposits to buy more Treasury securities after the transaction as it did before. In either case, the system never runs out of money – it never runs out of the capacity to buy more government debt.

Welcome to the world of monetary sovereignty!

Essentially, this is what proponents of Modern Monetary Theory (MMT) teach, although they explain it somewhat differently. With this monetary sovereignty, the government is not limited in its ability to fund spending through debt. And beyond this, the Federal Reserve stands ready as needed to immediately purchase Treasury debt from bank and dealer buyers. For those reasons, there will always be sufficient funds and sufficient buyers for the Treasury's debt.

Is There a Limit?

So, is there no limit to this? The US government debt-to-GDP ratio (including intragovernmental holdings) stood at 133 percent at the end of 2020, up from 108 percent in 2019. Could the public debt ratio go, unvexed, to as high as 150, 200, or 250 percent? If not, then why not, and what could or would go wrong? This is the enigma we need to understand.

Chart 9 shows the countries that have the highest public debt-to-GDP ratios as of 2019. Only Japan operates at a level above 200 percent today; however, when we peel back the onion, Japan – uniquely among major economies – has used a major portion of its debt to buy a significant amount of financial assets, equivalent to roughly 85 percent of GDP, so its *net* government debt is actually only approximately 154 percent. After making that adjustment,

Country	2019 Government Debt to GDP
Japan	239%
Greece	177%
Italy	132%
Portugal	118%
Singapore	114%
Source – CEIC data	

Chart 9

no country yet operates at the rarified level of 200-plus percent government debt to GDP. And among major countries, only Japan is adding government debt at a rate that may take it over 200 percent on a net basis anytime soon. (Note that Greece, Italy, and Portugal do not have monetary sovereignty because of their membership in the European Monetary Union and are thus constrained in their ability to deal with their high government debt.)

Could debt to GDP reach 250 percent or even 300 percent? Is there a government debt limit? This question of limits is rarely asked or examined in these terms, including by proponents of MMT, who view the emergence of inflation as the limit, rather than viewing the limit as a percentage of debt to GDP. The two most frequently cited adverse possibilities of a high government debt-to-GDP ratio are inflation and a large decline in the value of the dollar versus other major currencies. These two consequences are in some respects related. Let's examine them both.

The dollar may very well decline against other currencies, but in the past decade, as US government debt has exploded, it has declined modestly versus some and actually increased in value modestly versus others. A dollar decline is always a risk, but generally other major countries are in the same financial boat as the United States. It would be difficult for the dollar to fall much for this reason, because the rest of the developed world is also following the path of expanding debt and declining interest rates.

We have already examined the issue of inflation briefly, but it remains the big fear. In fact, proponents of MMT posit inflation as the signal that a limit in government deficit spending is approaching, and government deficit spending is no longer needed to boost employment.

With rising government deficits and debt, many believe the specter of inflation, even hyperinflation, might be just around the corner. But the evidence of the past forty years would indicate the opposite. In fact, based on that evidence, it is more reasonable to believe that the specter around the corner is simply more disinflation. Rising debt may thus do the very opposite of what has long been taught and feared.

From 1981 to 2019, while federal debt to GDP more than tripled, inflation dropped from 10 percent to 2 percent, and long-term Treasury interest rates fell in a spiky, uneven, but nevertheless descending path from 14 percent to 2 percent. (These trends have inevitably seen temporary reversals from time to time of over 100 basis points, and may now, but the core trend has remained downward.)

That is forty years of evidence that growing debt is part of what *causes* interest rates and inflation to go down, since a high burden of debt (especially private debt) stunts economic growth. And with higher levels of debt, interest rate increases have a magnified impact and thus have a greater economic braking effect; hence, in this way, greater levels of debt serve to keep interest rates low.

The Red Herring of Economics Debunked: Money Supply and Debt Growth Don't Cause Inflation

Economists have long had the notion that high money supply growth and high government debt growth are primary causes of inflation, yet there is little empirical support in modern, developed economies for this idea. The conclusion of our research is that rapid money supply growth is not a primary cause of inflation. Neither are rapid growth in government debt, declining interest rates, or rapid increases in a central bank's balance sheet.

These are easy propositions to test. We can analyze and then chart all countries where data are available, establish various thresholds of what we consider high money supply growth and high government debt growth, and then see how many times those instances were followed by high inflation. In a study we conducted in 2016, we developed a database of forty-seven countries that together constitute 91 percent of global GDP, and looked at each episode of rapid money supply growth to see if it was followed by high inflation. In the majority of cases, it was not. In fact, the opposite was true: a large percentage of the cases of high inflation were not preceded by high money supply growth. These forty-seven countries all rank within the top seventy largest economies as measured by GDP and include all of the top twenty countries. If a country was not included, it was because we could not get a sufficiently complete set of historical data on that country.

We looked at a variety of scenarios. In one case, we defined high M2 growth as 200 percent nominal growth in five years, and high inflation as a period of three consecutive years of 5 percent or more inflation. Of the thirty such high M2 growth periods, only eight led to high inflation and twenty-two did not. By contrast, there were forty-five instances of high inflation that were not preceded by this high M2 growth. There was no positive correlation and may perhaps have been a negative one.

To many, the idea that rapid money supply growth brings inflation *seems* true. But history does not bear that out.

These results did not change appreciably when we divided our test cases into large, medium, or small countries. Nor if we used high growth in government debt instead of high money supply growth.

We have done this analysis using a variety of thresholds for money supply growth and government debt growth. We have also done it analyzing such factors as declining interest rates and increasing central bank size to assess whether those factors caused inflation. None of them was a predictor of inflation. Our analysis would suggest that it is not even close. The results can be viewed in an article I published on the Evonomics website (see Works Cited). Chart 10 provides a synopsis of some of these results.

This notion of inflation caused by money supply or debt growth is one of the great red herrings of economics. The fact is that, other things being

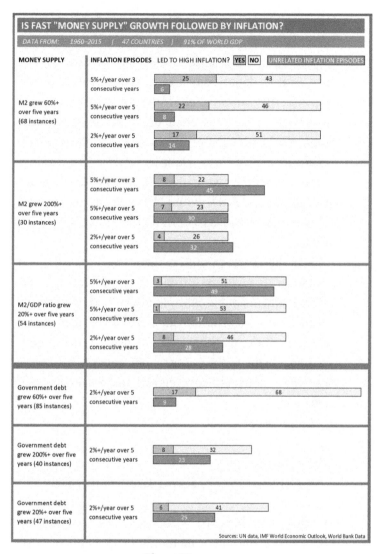

IS FAST "MONEY SUPPLY" GROWTH FOLLOWED BY INFLATION?

DATA FROM: 1960–2015 | 47 COUNTRIES | 91% OF WORLD GDP

MONEY SUPPLY	INFLATION EPISODES	LED TO HIGH INFLATION? YES NO	UNRELATED INFLATION EPISODES
M2 grew 60%+ over five years (68 instances)	5%+/year over 3 consecutive years	YES 25 / NO 43	6
	5%+/year over 5 consecutive years	YES 22 / NO 46	8
	2%+/year over 5 consecutive years	YES 17 / NO 51	14
M2 grew 200%+ over five years (30 instances)	5%+/year over 3 consecutive years	YES 8 / NO 22	45
	5%+/year over 5 consecutive years	YES 7 / NO 23	30
	2%+/year over 5 consecutive years	YES 4 / NO 26	32
M2/GDP ratio grew 20%+ over five years (54 instances)	5%+/year over 3 consecutive years	YES 3 / NO 51	49
	5%+/year over 5 consecutive years	YES 1 / NO 53	37
	2%+/year over 5 consecutive years	YES 8 / NO 46	28
Government debt grew 60%+ over five years (85 instances)	2%+/year over 5 consecutive years	YES 17 / NO 68	9
Government debt grew 200%+ over five years (40 instances)	2%+/year over 5 consecutive years	YES 8 / NO 32	23
Government debt grew 20%+ over five years (47 instances)	2%+/year over 5 consecutive years	YES 6 / NO 41	25

Sources: UN data, IMF World Economic Outlook, World Bank Data

Chart 10

equal, high levels of debt appear to be disinflation-ary, or even deflationary, and I surmise this is in part because they suppress consumption and investment, and thus weaken aggregate demand. As mentioned, high levels of debt deepen the economic braking effect of higher rates. Debt to GDP levels are now double what they were in 1980, so a 100-basis-point rise in interest rates would choke economic growth as much as a 200-basis-point rise would have back then.

We therefore cannot realistically look to price inflation to solve the problem of high debt, either. These data would seem to lend credence to theories such as post-Keynesianism and MMT that argue there is little drawback to higher levels of gov-ernment debt for a country like the United States that has monetary sovereignty and issues its own currency.

Or is there?

Consequences of Rising Government Debt

I posit that there are two consequences to rising debt that economists, including proponents of post-Keynesianism and MMT, don't contemplate, and that suggest a limit on how high the government debt-to-GDP ratio can go. I would submit that over the long term that limit will come not from higher inflation, but instead from ever-lower inflation and interest rates (perhaps even negative rates), ever-rising inequality, and ever-deepening social polarization.

One consequence of rising government debt has been worsening inequality. Recall that the issuance of government debt creates private sector wealth. Rising government debt increases inequality because the government spending that creates this wealth has disproportionately gone to the wealthy, including companies and their shareholders in such industries as defense, healthcare, and construction. (Of course, growing debt could be spent in such a way as to reverse inequality, but that would require a radically different direction in spending.)

An additional consequence seems very much to be declining interest rates themselves, which also feed into rising inequality. A decline in interest rates is the very opposite of what textbooks on economics taught us to expect. In some markets, these rates have reached zero or even turned negative. The trends in the United States, China, Japan, and the major European countries all show exactly the same long-term downward trend in interest rates (as seen in Charts 1 through 5).

Declining interest rates sound like an obvious social good, and perhaps the post-Keynesian and MMT theorists are therefore correct that high government debt need not worry us. If it causes declining interest rates, then that sounds like a benefit. Negative interest rates, for example, if they were ever pervasive enough, would be a form of jubilee, since they result in a *de facto* reduction in debt outstanding.

Things are more complicated than that, however. The drawback to declining interest rates is that they bring an overallocation and misallocation of investments that, in turn, increases asset bubbles: the rapid rise in the price of certain assets; most notably, real estate and stocks. With low interest rates, things like money market funds and certificates of deposit have very low yields, and so investors increasingly move to real estate, stocks, and other riskier investments in search of higher returns, and that inflow of investment drives up their values. Thus, while low rates don't bring price inflation, they do bring asset value inflation. Since the top 10 percent of the US population owns almost 60 percent of real estate, stocks, and bonds, the average American holds comparatively few of these assets, and low rates boost their value, this further widens the financial gulf between the haves and the have-less.

In addition, for moderate- and lower-income groups, especially retirees, who live off of their savings, lower rates mean lower income from safer investments such as certificates of deposit, government bonds, and money market funds. With their income thus reduced, these individuals either downsize their lives or seek inappropriately risky investments, or both.

This effect will persist even if interest rates and inflation decline no further.

Furthermore, even those moderate- and lower-income groups who do borrow get little benefit from these low rates, because lenders do not fully offer them those rates, in part due to the high operating costs and higher risks associated with smaller loans. Instead, they pay interest rates of 20 percent, 30 percent, 60 percent, or more on their unsecured loans.

And rising government debt does mean that as a practical consequence of actual legislative behavior, government spending gets diverted from other programs to pay interest, and this can lead to more tax dollars to service increased spending. All of this suggests that there are practical limits on the government debt-to-GDP ratio, and the problem does need to be dealt with overtly, somehow, rather than ignored.

The Enigma of Government Debt

Can the Government Create Money Without Debt?

We have motivation and reason, then, to find ways to moderate the levels of government debt in relation to GDP, but the solutions are not immediately obvious. As I've reviewed here, we can't simply wipe it out, since most government debt is held by individual investors, pension funds, and the Social Security Trust Fund, rather than foreign governments. Canceling it, as some have suggested, would wipe out a significant part of US household net worth, impair the government's ability to borrow in the future, and increase the rate it would pay on any such debt.

But what if there were a way for the government to create money without simultaneously creating a commensurate amount of government debt – at least government debt in the sense that it pays interest, has a maturity, and therefore ultimately has to be redeemed?

There is.

To find precedents for just such a thing, we need only take a brief detour into America's own monetary past. The most prominent example comes from the Legal Tender Acts of the 1860s. To help fund the Civil War, Congress authorized the issuance of $450 million in new bills, which came to be known as "greenbacks." This was just one of many instances and types of money creation in early US history.

The government issued a significant quantity of greenbacks, totaling more than 5 percent of GDP and 14 percent of the cost of the Civil War, given that GDP reached over $8 billion and the total cost of the war was $3.3 billion. From the end of the Civil War in 1865 until gold convertibility was restored in 1879, an average of roughly $350 million greenbacks were in circulation. Of course, greenbacks paid no interest and had no maturity. They gained acceptance as people realized that they could be used to pay taxes. (Notably, during most of that postwar span, the US economy experienced deflation, not inflation.)

We could do the paperless equivalent of this today by having the Treasury issue certificates that do not pay interest and do not have maturities. This would be a modern-day counterpart to the Legal Tender Acts that created greenbacks. *Instruments that pay no interest and have no maturity are more like capital than debt.* They are perpetual. So let's call these new certificates US Treasury Perpetual Certificates.

The Federal Reserve would buy these Perpetual Certificates by crediting the Treasury's account at the

Fed. The accounting entries at the Federal Reserve would be an increase in Perpetual Certificates, an asset held by the Fed, and an increase to the Treasury's account, which is a liability of the Fed. The Treasury could then spend this money from this account in the private sector, creating deposits.

The Treasury might issue and spend with Perpetuals similar to how it spends with conventional Treasury issuance, but Perpetuals do not go in the same liability category on the balance sheet as conventional Treasury bonds (see Appendix Charts D). Without the obligation to pay interest and without a redemption or maturity, Perpetuals behave more like equity than debt. So I have given them their own category – Perpetuals – and since they do not ever come due and therefore cannot be redeemed, I have not subtracted them from assets in calculating the Treasury's net worth as I have with conventional Treasury securities. With Perpetuals, the Treasury's debt would be less than with a conventional Treasury issuance, and its net worth would thus be higher (compare the final chart in Appendix Charts B and D).

This idea is not only akin to the issuance of greenbacks but also in keeping with the trillion-dollar coin idea suggested by Rohan Grey and other adherents of MMT, an idea that gained popularity in the early 1990s and then resurged around the "debt ceiling" crises of the 2000s. Essentially, they propose that the Treasury mint one coin worth $1 trillion and send it to the Federal Reserve to replenish the Treasury's account there.

I would advocate Perpetuals only for large, developed economies with significantly more stability than smaller or lesser developed countries, which contend with different issues.

Perpetuals would create money without creating government debt, at least in the sense of debt that pays interest and has a maturity. That is a key, and profound, difference. A Perpetuals initiative would improve the ratio of GDP to government debt that does pay interest and have a maturity. It would obviate talk of burdening future generations with this debt. Because of these characteristics, Perpetuals could indeed more accurately be referred to as an act of "printing money out of thin air" – just as this appropriately characterizes greenbacks authorized by the Legal Tender Acts.

Perpetuals, in short, would create *non-government-debt-based money*. Let's refine the terminology and call it *perpetual money*. This would allow us to escape the conundrum created by the relationship of debt, money, and economic growth that I've described throughout this book.

121

If we were to issue $1 trillion in Perpetuals in 2021 in lieu of an equivalent amount of conventional Treasury securities, by our estimate the government debt-to-GDP ratio at the end of 2021 would be roughly 125–30 percent instead of 130–5 percent. If we were to issue that much for each of five years starting in 2021 – again, in lieu of an equivalent amount of conventional securities – the likely ratio to GDP at year end 2025 would be 115–20 percent instead of 135–40 percent.

Earlier I estimated that the cost of my proposed jubilee programs would be high but manageable. That would be especially true if we used Perpetuals for parts of the plan where government is asked to assume the debt. In fact, Perpetuals are ideally suited for just such specialized needs as jubilee programs, Covid-19-related stimulus, and the stimulus strategy referred to as "helicopter money." The term "helicopter money" means different things to different people, but most often refers to programs where the government issues checks broadly as a form of stimulus, such as the $1,200 checks dispensed in the 2020 CARES Act. If conventional Treasury securities fund the helicopter money, then it increases US government debt. If Perpetuals fund the helicopter money, then it does not.

The Enigma of Government Debt

Is It Dangerous to Create Perpetual Money?

Perpetuals can be a powerful mechanism to correct our economic course, but the idea is not a debt panacea. Everything has a downside, including Perpetuals. It may very well be that the downside is inflation. We have already argued that, contrary to received wisdom, issuing more government debt, even with any resulting increase in the money supply, has led to lower inflation. But I believe that this has held true in the past partly because the interest rate obligation and maturity aspect of Treasury securities act as accountability mechanisms. Those securities require that interest be paid every six months and make principal fully due at a specific point in time. Perpetuals do not have those same accountability mechanisms, or discipline. In the eighteenth century, those responsible for funding the American Revolution understood this difference: in that war's waning but crucial last two years, they created the Bank of North America, the first true bank in the country, to have a source for bank loans for war spending in lieu of the printed money they'd been using so liberally. Those loans had an accountability that printed money did not.

We might justifiably worry, then, that the creation of money without interest rate or maturity – and the money supply growth linked to this phenomenon – is a different and particular type of money creation that would indeed lead to inflation, in contrast to our earlier discussion of conventional money supply growth.

But to address this concern of inflation, we can simply limit the use of Perpetuals – the key to avoiding inflation with Perpetuals would come down to volume. It may very well be a linear relationship: the more non-debt-based money, the more inflation. Low amounts of something like greenbacks or Perpetuals would result in little if any inflation; medium amounts – say, 25 percent to 50 percent of GDP – would bring moderate inflation; and high amounts – say, 50 to 100 percent of GDP for several consecutive years – would bring higher inflation. The correct titration of Perpetuals into the money stream would limit the threat of inflation.

Yet a modestly higher level of inflation might not be that bad a thing at this time, when some central banks have been trying to kindle it with limited success. Perhaps we need a little inflation. After all, even slight inflation could slightly erode the burden of debt.

The bottom line is that we should be judicious in the issuance of Perpetuals. To do this, we should impose some legislative limits: for example, a cap on issuance of 5 percent of GDP in any one year with a cumulative cap of 25 percent of GDP.

* * *

We need a balance between debt-based money and perpetual money. It may be that such a balance is the healthier and more technically sound way of managing monetary policy in today's world rather than simply relying on debt-based money.

But isn't the creation of perpetual money heresy in a country where money creation is theoretically so tightly controlled?

Absolutely not. Alternative forms of money and currency creation may be vilified today but, historically, from the time the US Constitution was adopted until well into the nineteenth century, the United States had a much greater variety of methods for money creation. The creation of money through greenbacks is an important and familiar example, but is just one of many. In fact, for much of the country's financial history, including periods of its greatest growth, the United States didn't even have a currency, and most certainly did not have a monopoly on the money created and used in its economy. In the earliest decades, a fascinating and very high-growth time in US monetary history, banks created most of the currency used in the economy, dispensing it as the proceeds of loans.

The Treasury issued debt, and occasionally some of that was used explicitly as currency (even though the government was often loath to call it that). At other times, companies, institutions, and even individuals issued the equivalent of currency. Money was also created when individuals took silver and gold to the US Mint to make coins for use as money.

The important point to note is that the United States did just fine in the nineteenth century with this heterodoxy of currencies, growing to become the world's largest economy and rarely experiencing any meaningful inflation, except during war.

Far from an economic or policy heresy, different forms of money creation have an extensive precedent in the United States. If we don't consider Perpetuals because it seems too "radical" an idea, then that would reveal our lack of knowledge about our own monetary past.

Epilogue

Concluding Thoughts

This book has described the world we are moving toward, with a continuation of the staggering growth of debt and its pernicious impact – what some would call the "Japanification" of America, characterized by sky-high debt levels and desultory growth. We have seen that this debt growth is no accident, but an intrinsic feature of the system that will persist without overt interventions, and that the burden of this debt is suffered most widely by average Americans. We have seen that debt levels are extremely difficult to reduce, absent broad-based and thoughtful initiatives on debt restructuring, and have shown why the most common beliefs about how to reduce debt will not work.

We have outlined certain initiatives for debt relief, both discrete and ongoing, grouped under the term "jubilee," with ways to build this debt relief into the very architecture and machinery of the economy.

In a sense, we need to expand and extend debt restructuring opportunities to households similar to those that corporate America has long enjoyed, and provide more and better ways to restructure and renegotiate contracts for individuals. This would make jubilee a more normal aspect of economic function, and not a quixotic hope.

* * *

A brief additional word on limits.

The pages of this book so far have taken as a given the need for GDP growth. Indeed, the assumption that we can and should grow 2 to 3 percent per year indefinitely has informed thought and policy in government and business for well over 100 years.

But that represents a radical change in human history. For thousands of years, from the Roman Empire and the Renaissance all the way until the early 1800s, annual global GDP growth was very close to zero. Then came the steam engine and the proliferation of banks and the Industrial Revolution, and growth skyrocketed. Human achievement flourished, as did new dilemmas ranging from pollution to community disruption.

This book has argued that GDP growth is centrally related to private sector debt growth, so I do not view it as a coincidence that a proliferation of banks accompanied the Industrial Revolution and its remarkable acceleration of GDP growth. Around 1780, few banks existed in France, Austria, the Netherlands, or the principalities that would constitute Germany, and effectively none existed in the United States, but by 1850 there were hundreds. More did exist in Britain in 1780, as the country was on the leading edge of banking, but its number, too, mushroomed in the early 1800s.

In the last 200 years, with radical innovations in technology and this explosion of banking, GDP increased over seventy-fold and per capita GDP increased a remarkable eleven times.

Many assume that history will and should continue on this trajectory, but there is an alternative view. Giorgos Kallis and his coauthors in their important and provocative book *The Case for Degrowth* advocate moving away from the relentless drive for more:

The obvious axiom that nothing can grow indefinitely was disregarded in the twentieth century when desire for perpetual growth became a guiding force in economics, science, and across political ideologies. Companies, banks, economists, and governments developed operational strategies that depended on continually growing profits and GDPs. . . . Participants in these processes came to perceive perpetual growth as natural and right. But there is nothing natural in perpetual growth. . . . 3 percent annual growth doubles an economy every twenty-four years, quadruples it in forty-eight, growing sixteen-fold in a century . . . [in] a global economy that already extracts 92 billion tons of materials annually.

Not to mention that this growth is dependent on a commensurate or greater growth in debt.

These advocates view the current pace of growth as an unsustainable trend that will bring more bad than good and the risk of collapse.

For advocates of degrowth, I would strongly argue that this need for a jubilee strategy is just as acute as, if not more so than, for those who advocate growth. The objective of the degrowth movement is, as Kallis, et al. argue, to "produce and consume differently, and less . . . to share more and distribute more fairly while the pie shrinks . . . [and] to do so in ways that support pleasurable and meaningful lives." As it now stands, the mass of extant debt would strangle these nascent degrowth hopes, because while the economic pie in degrowth would shrink, the debt pie would not, meaning that the debt-to-GDP ratio would escalate rapidly. In fact, while the economic pie was shrinking, debt would be constant or growing because of the compounding effects of interest. Successful degrowth, then, would require a debt amnesty strategy – as does successful continued growth.

The Opportunity Before Us

The initiatives proposed in this book will have a liberating and energizing effect on the economy and reduce inequality. Lower debt levels will measurably improve the lives of millions of Americans. All stand to gain. Households will be stronger. Governments, businesses, and financial institutions will be better off *because* households will be stronger, and more able to allocate money toward consumption, investment, and key purchases rather than debt service and repayment. The economic engine will simply run better – not just for the wealthiest but for all.

There are modern-day precedents for jubilee. The United States and its Allies restructured or forgave public and private debt in Germany after World War II, and that action paved the way for Germany's postwar economic miracle.

The aftermath of Covid-19, with our collective need to repair the economic damage brought by the virus and begin the rocky and steep climb back, provides an opportunity to think deeply and act creatively on debt matters. Through 2020 and early 2021, the Covid-19 struggle brought new layers of debt, with US private and public sector debt rising sharply from their pre-Covid-19 levels.

This pandemic at least temporarily deprived a large group of citizens of the opportunity to earn a living through no fault of their own – those in the restaurant, travel, and service industries, and many more. Unlike the great financial crisis of 2008, Covid-19-related debt growth has not come from those who got into debt because of their own folly. Politically, this may provide a more palatable context for jubilee.

Jubilee can be structured in a way that is fundamentally positive for all involved. The banks and other lenders will win because they will have an effective way of dealing with troubled loans already on their books. Businesses will win through the improved financial wellbeing of their customers. Families and individuals will win because a key source of their struggles and stress will diminish. Advocates of a more expansive jubilee will win because at least some of their hopes will be realized. Those who are concerned about rising government debt will win because jubilee will utilize a fresh avenue for funding programs not dependent on new government debt.

The political benefits of this program could be significant to any politician with the commitment to bring forward legislation to enact it: increased growth, relief to many voters, and palatable costs not overly burdensome to business or government. For the current Democratic administration, it could be a rallying cry to unite the party.

The jubilee initiatives that this book has described would accomplish what has never been accomplished in recent economic history: they would arrest the otherwise inexorable rise in the debt-to-GDP ratio while avoiding calamity and spurring growth.

This is the opportunity before us.

Appendix

Chart A

Bank Lending

Financial assets and liabilities only

Starting Point

Betty Smith				Bank MNO			
Assets			**Liabilities**		**Assets**		**Liabilities**
Acct. at Bank MNO	$0					B. Smith Account	$0
		Net Worth	($0)			**Net Worth**	$0

The moment before the Bank MNO loan
• At the moment before the loan, Betty Smith has an account at Bank MNO, but no money in it.
• This is a transaction between Betty and Bank MNO; the Treasury, the Federal Reserve, and any other bank do not play a role (until Betty uses this account to pay others, which is not shown in this example).

Bank Lending

Loan Funding Completed

Betty Smith				Bank MNO			
Assets			**Liabilities**		**Assets**		**Liabilities**
Acct. at Bank MNO	$1,000,000	Loan from Bank MNO	$1,000,000	Loan to B. Smith	$1,000,000	B. Smith Account	$1,000,000
		Net Worth	$0			**Net Worth**	$0

134

Appendix

Chart B

Treasury Bond Issuance and Related Spending

Financial assets and liabilities only

These are the simplified hypothetical balance sheets of the relevant entities before and after the issuance of an additional $1 million to pay Betty Smith for consulting services. This is the specific case in which a bank purchases the Treasury security.

Starting Point

US Treasury				Federal Reserve Bank			
	Assets		**Liabilities**		**Assets**		**Liabilities**
Fed. Reserve Acct.	$0	T-Bonds- Fed	$1,000,000	US Treasury Bonds	$1,000,000	Bank XYZ Account	$1,000,000
		T-Bonds- Bank XYZ	$1,000,000			Treasury Account	$0
		T-Bonds- Total	$2,000,000			Bank MNO Account	$0
		Net Worth	($2,000,000)			**Net Worth**	$0

Bank XYZ				Bank MNO			
	Assets		**Liabilities**		**Assets**		**Liabilities**
US Treasury Bonds	$1,000,000			Fed. Reserve Acct.	$0	B. Smith Account	$0
Fed. Reserve Acct.	$1,000,000						
		Net Worth	$2,000,000			**Net Worth**	$0

Betty Smith				The moment before the new Treasury borrowing
	Assets		**Liabilities**	
Acct. at Bank MNO	$0			• Betty Smith has an account at Bank MNO, but no money in it.
				• This hypothetical Treasury has a negative financial net worth, which is also true for the actual US Treasury, whose net worth as of 12/31/2019 was negative $22.9 trillion.
		Net Worth	$0	

Treasury Bond Issuance and Related Spending

Financial assets and liabilities only

Step 1: Treasury Issues $1 Million in Debt

US Treasury				Federal Reserve Bank			
	Assets		**Liabilities**		**Assets**		**Liabilities**
Fed. Reserve Acct.	$1,000,000	T-Bonds- Fed	$1,000,000	US Treasury Bonds	$1,000,000	Bank XYZ Account	$0
		T-Bonds- Bank XYZ	$2,000,000			Treasury Account	$1,000,000
		T-Bonds- Total	$3,000,000			Bank MNO Account	$0
		Net Worth	($2,000,000)			**Net Worth**	$0

Appendix

Bank XYZ			
Assets			**Liabilities**
US Treasury Bonds	$2,000,000		
Fed. Reserve Acct.	$0		
		Net Worth	$2,000,000

Bank MNO			
Assets			**Liabilities**
Fed. Reserve Acct.		$0	B. Smith Account	$0
		Net Worth	$0

Betty Smith			
Assets			**Liabilities**
Acct. at Bank MNO	$0		
		Net Worth	$0

Treasury sells $1 million in T-Bonds to Bank XYZ

- Bank XYZ's holding of Treasury bonds increases by $1 million, but the balance in its Fed account decreases by $1 million to pay for it.
- The Treasury's account at the Fed increases by $1 million as it gets paid by Bank XYZ for the bonds.

Treasury Bond Issuance and Related Spending

Financial assets and liabilities only

Step 2: Treasury Pays Vendor $1 Million

US Treasury			
Assets			**Liabilities**
Fed. Reserve Acct.	$0	T-Bonds- Fed	$1,000,000
		T-Bonds- Bank XYZ	$2,000,000
		T-Bonds- Total	$3,000,000
		Net Worth	($3,000,000)

Federal Reserve Bank			
Assets			**Liabilities**
US Treasury Bonds	$1,000,000	Bank XYZ Account	$0
		Treasury Account	$0
		Bank MNO Account	$1,000,000
		Net Worth	$0

Bank XYZ			
Assets			**Liabilities**
US Treasury Bonds	$2,000,000		
Fed. Reserve Acct.	$0		
		Net Worth	$2,000,000

Bank MNO			
Assets			**Liabilities**
Fed. Reserve Acct.	$1,000,000	B. Smith Account	$1,000,000
		Net Worth	$0

Betty Smith			
Assets			**Liabilities**
Acct. at Bank MNO	$1,000,000		
		Net Worth	$1,000,000

Treasury pays B. Smith $1 million for consulting services

- Betty receives a check for $1 million from the Treasury. That check is drawn on the Treasury's account at the Federal Reserve.
- Bank MNO credits Betty's account for that $1 million and makes a claim on the Treasury's Federal Reserve account for that amount.
- The Treasury's Fed account decreases by $1 million as its money is transferred into the Fed account of Betty's bank MNO.
- Betty's net worth increases by $1 million, and the Treasury's decreases by $1 million.

Appendix

Note: The payment to Betty is only an addition to deposits if these Treasury securities end up owned and held by the Federal Reserve or a bank. In the case where a person or other non-bank private sector entity buys the Treasury security, which is more often the greater amount, private sector deposits are used to buy the security, then restored when the government spends the proceeds, so the total amount of deposits remains the same.

Chart C

Federal Reserve Open Market Operations

Financial assets and liabilities only

Starting Point

US Treasury		
Assets		**Liabilities**
	T-Bonds- Fed	$1,000,000
	T-Bonds- Bank XYZ	$1,000,000
	Net Worth	($2,000,000)

Federal Reserve Bank			
Assets			**Liabilities**
US Treasury Bonds	$1,000,000	Bank XYZ Account	$1,000,000
		Net Worth	$0

Bank XYZ		
Assets		**Liabilities**
US Treasury Bonds	$1,000,000	
Fed. Reserve Acct.	$1,000,000	
	Net Worth	$2,000,000

The moment before the Fed's OMO
• This is a transaction that occurs directly between the Federal Reserve and a given bank, which, in this hypothetical, is Bank XYZ.
• The Federal Reserve Bank has $1 million in assets (US Treasury bonds) and $1 million in liabilities (Bank XYZ's Fed account).
• For simplicity, in this example the Fed has a net worth of $0, but the actual Fed has a positive net worth.

Appendix

Federal Reserve Open Market Operations

Financial assets and liabilities only

Fed Buys $1 Million in US Treasury Bonds from Bank XYZ

US Treasury		
Assets		**Liabilities**
	T-Bonds- Fed	$2,000,000
	T-Bonds- Bank XYZ	$0
	Net Worth	($2,000,000)

Federal Reserve Bank			
Assets			**Liabilities**
US Treasury Bonds	$2,000,000	Bank XYZ Account	$2,000,000
		Net Worth	$0

Bank XYZ		
Assets		**Liabilities**
US Treasury Bonds	$0	
Fed. Reserve Acct.	$2,000,000	
	Net Worth	$2,000,000

After OMO
• Bank XYZ has $1 million in additional reserves from proceeds of the Treasury bond sale.
• Federal Reserve assets and liabilities both increase by $1 million through the addition of $1 million in Treasury bonds and $1 million more in Bank XYZ's Federal Reserves account.

Note: The new Treasury security asset at the Fed is accompanied by a new reserve, which is a liability of the Fed, though technically no new deposits have been created. When the Fed buys Treasury securities from non-banks, it does create deposits.

The Fed performs OMO in part to lower rates and encourage more lending, although its efficacy in this regard is debated. Reserves, while not deposits, are a specialized liability, or debt, of the Fed that in essence serve as deposits for the banking industry – kept at the Fed to settle payments between banks, buy bonds, and meet regulatory requirements.

Beginning in 2008, this OMO activity increased and included purchases of Treasury securities from non-bank entities in what was termed "quantitative easing."

Appendix

Chart D

Treasury Perpetual Issuance and Related Spending

Financial assets and liabilities only

These are the simplified hypothetical balance sheets of the relevant entities before and after the issuance of $1 million in Perpetual Certificates to pay Betty Smith for consulting services.

Starting Point

US Treasury			
Assets			**Liabilities**
Fed Account	$0	T-Bonds- Fed	$1,000,000
		T-Bonds- Bank XYZ	$1,000,000
		T-Bonds- Total	$2,000,000
		Net Worth	($2,000,000)

Federal Reserve Bank			
	Assets		**Liabilities**
US Treasury Bonds	$1,000,000	Bank XYZ Account	$1,000,000
		Net Worth	$0

Bank XYZ			
	Assets		**Liabilities**
US Treasury Bonds	$1,000,000		
Fed. Reserve Acct.	$1,000,000		
		Net Worth	$2,000,000

Bank MNO			
	Assets		**Liabilities**
		B. Smith Account	$0
		Net Worth	$0

Betty Smith		
	Assets	**Liabilities**
Acct. at Bank MNO	$0	
	Net Worth	$0

The moment before new Perpetual Issuance
• Betty Smith has an account at Bank MNO, but no money in it.
• This hypothetical Treasury has a negative financial net worth, which is also true of the actual US Treasury, whose net worth as of 12/31/2019 was negative $22.9 trillion.

Treasury Perpetual Issuance and Related Spending

Financial assets and liabilities only

Alternative Step 1: Treasury Issues $1 Million in Perpetual Certificates

US Treasury			
Assets			**Liabilities**
Fed Account	$1,000,000	T-Bonds- Fed	$1,000,000
		T-Bonds- Bank XYZ	$1,000,000
		T-Bonds- Total	$2,000,000
		Perpetual Issued	$1,000,000
		Net Worth	($1,000,000)

Federal Reserve Bank			
	Assets		**Liabilities**
US Treasury Bonds	$1,000,000	Bank XYZ Account	$1,000,000
US Perpetual Bonds	$1,000,000	Treasury Account	$1,000,000
		Net Worth	$0

Bank XYZ			
	Assets		**Liabilities**
US Treasury Bonds	$1,000,000		
Fed. Reserve Acct.	$1,000,000		
		Net Worth	$2,000,000

Bank MNO			
	Assets		**Liabilities**
		B. Smith Account	$0
		Net Worth	$0

139

Appendix

Betty Smith		
Assets		**Liabilities**
Acct. at Bank MNO	$0	
	Net Worth	$0

Treasury issues $1 million in Perpetuals to Fed
• The Federal Reserve buys $1 million in Perpetual Certificates, and thus its holding of Perpetual Certificates increases by $1 million, which it pays for by crediting the Treasury's Fed account.
• The Treasury's net worth increases by $1 million as the Perpetual is counted toward net worth, and not subtracted as a conventional liability.

Treasury Perpetual Issuance and Related Spending

Financial assets and liabilities only

Alternative Step 2: Treasury Spends the $1 million from Perpetual Certificate Issuance

US Treasury			
Assets			**Liabilities**
Fed Account	$0	T-Bonds- Fed	$1,000,000
		T-Bonds- Bank XYZ	$1,000,000
		T-Bonds- Total	$2,000,000
		Perpetual Issued	$1,000,000
		Net Worth	($2,000,000)

Federal Reserve Bank			
Assets			**Liabilities**
US Treasury Bonds	$1,000,000	Bank XYZ Account	$1,000,000
US Perpetual Bond	$1,000,000	Treasury Account	$0
		Bank MNO Account	$1,000,000
		Net Worth	$0

Bank XYZ			
Assets			**Liabilities**
US Treasury Bonds	$1,000,000		
Fed. Reserve Acct.	$1,000,000		
		Net Worth	$2,000,000

Bank MNO			
Assets			**Liabilities**
Account at Fed	$1,000,000	B. Smith Account	$1,000,000
		Net Worth	$0

Betty Smith		
Assets		**Liabilities**
Acct. at Bank MNO	$1,000,000	
	Net Worth	$1,000,000

Treasury pays B. Smith $1 million for consulting services
• Betty receives a check for $1 million from the Treasury. That check is drawn on the Treasury's account at the Federal Reserve.
• Bank MNO credits Betty's account for that $1 million and makes a claim on the Treasury's Federal Reserve account for that amount.
• The Treasury's Fed account decreases by $1 million as its money is transferred into the Fed account of Betty's bank MNO.
• Smith's net worth increases by $1 million; Treasury's decreases by $1 million, but it is still greater than Chart B, Step 2.

Works Cited

Collins, Sara R., Munira Z. Gunja, and Gabriella N. Aboulafia. "Findings from the Commonwealth Fund Biennial Health Insurance Survey, 2020: US Health Insurance Coverage in 2020: A Looming Crisis in Affordability." *The Commonwealth Fund Issue Briefs*, August 19, 2020. *https://www.common wealthfund.org/publications/issue-briefs/2020/aug/loo ming-crisis-health-coverage-2020-biennial.*

Consumer Financial Protection Bureau. "Consumer Credit Reports: A Study of Medical and Non-Medical Collections." *Research and Reports*, December 2014. *https://files.consumerfinance.gov/f/201412_cfpb_re ports_consumer-credit-medical-and-non-medical-col lections.pdf.*

Graeber, David. *Debt: The First 5,000 Years.* Brooklyn, NY: Melville House, 2011.

Grey, Rohan. "Administering Money: Coinage, Debt Crises, and the Future of Fiscal Policy." *SSRN*, February

11, 2020. *https://papers.ssrn.com/sol3/papers.cfm?ab stract_id=3536440.*

Hamel, Liz, Mira Norton, Karen Pollitz, Larry Levitt, Gary Claxton, and Mollyann Brodie. "The Burden of Medical Debt: Results from the Kaiser Family Foundation/New York Times Medical Bills Survey." The Henry K. Kaiser Family Foundation, January 5, 2016. *https://www.kff.org/wp-content/ uploads/2016/01/8806-the-burden-of-medical-debt- results-from-the-kaiser-family-foundation-new-york- times-medical-bills-survey.pdf.*

Hudson, Michael. *... and Forgive Them Their Debts: Lending, Foreclosure and Redemption from Bronze Age Finance to the Jubilee Year.* Dresden: ISLET-Verlag, 2018.

Jacoby, Jeff. "A Student Debt Bailout Would Be Unjust." *Boston Globe*, November 22, 2020. *https:// www.bostonglobe.com/2020/11/22/opinion/student- debt-bailout-would-be-unjust/.*

Kallis, Giorgos, Susan Paulson, Giacomo D'Alisa, and Federico Demaria. *The Case for Degrowth.* Cambridge: Polity, 2020.

Keen, Steve. "Discussing a Modern Debt Jubilee." Steve Keen's Debtwatch, December 19, 2020. *https://www.debtdeflation.com/blogs/2020/12/19/ discussing-a-modern-debt-jubilee-on-macroncheese/.*

Mankiw, Gregory N. *Macroeconomics.* New York: Worth Publishers, 2018.

Works Cited

Milgrom, Jacob. *Leviticus: A Book of Ritual and Ethics.* Minneapolis: Fortress Press, 2004.

Milgrom, Jacob. *Leviticus 1–16.* London: Yale University Press, 1998.

Milgrom, Jacob. *Leviticus 17–22.* London: Yale University Press, 2000.

Stiglitz, Joseph E. and Mark Zandi. "The One Housing Solution Left: Mass Mortgage Refinancing." *The New York Times*, August 12, 2012. *https://www.nytimes.com/2012/08/13/opinion/the-one-housing-solution-left-mass-mortgage-refinancing.html.*

Taylor, Astra. "How the Biden Administration Can Free Americans from Student Debt." *The New Yorker*, November 23, 2020. *https://www.newyorker.com/news/essay/how-the-biden-administration-can-free-americans-from-student-debt.*

Vague, Richard. "Rapid Money Supply Growth Does Not Cause Inflation." Evonomics, January 16, 2017. *https://evonomics.com/moneysupply/.*

Warren, Elizabeth. "Fixing Our Bankruptcy System to Give People a Second Chance." Warren Democrats. *https://elizabethwarren.com/plans/bankruptcy-reform.*